ELTON JOHN & BERNIE TAUPIN
THE COMPLETE LYRICS

ELTON JOHN BERNIE TAUPIN

THE COMPLETE LYRICS

PAVILION

First published in Great Britain in 1994 by
PAVILION BOOKS LIMITED
26 Upper Ground, London SE1 9PD

Song credits / Illustration credits appear on pages 188-192

Designed by Wherefore Art?

A CIP catalogue record for this book
is available from the British Library.

ISBN 1 85793 2722

Printed and bound in Singapore by Imago

2 4 6 8 10 9 7 5 3 1

This book may be ordered by post
direct from the publisher. Please contact
the Marketing Department.
But try your bookshop first.

Back cover photograph: Herb Ritts

FOREWORD

Elton John and Bernie Taupin's songwriting partnership has been an extraordinarily successful one which began in the most mundane of circumstances via an ad in the *New Musical Express* in 1967. Ever since then Elton has taken Bernie's finished lyrics away to inspire his accompanying music. Despite not collaborating in the sense of sitting in the same room, the achievements of this songwriting relationship are some of the most famous songs of our time: 'Candle in the Wind', 'Philadelphia Freedom', 'Goodbye Yellow Brick Road', 'Sacrifice', 'Sorry Seems To Be The Hardest Word'.

From the early beginnings in Americana to the most recent social commentaries, Bernie's lyrics encompass a wealth of subject matter in a richly poetic form. Elton's music brings a particular interpretation to these words, sometimes producing a song of intense pathos; at others a tremendous rock anthem. This book further shows how overflowing the lyrics are with associations – images, ideas, opinions – and how open they are, like poetry, to the reader's understanding. The art reproduced here is one more way of reading Bernie's lyrics and appreciating Elton's recordings. With photographs tracing the partnership from its early years right up to the present, and with visual pieces from contemporary artists both famous and unknown, this collection reinforces the strength of this songwriting team's work.

That this relationship has lasted almost three decades and produced such consistently exciting work, work which continues to develop and to challenge, is a testament to the huge talents of Elton John and Bernie Taupin.

Tim Rice
20 July 1994

act of war

This ain't no battle honey, this ain't no fight
How come you take it so hard when I stay out all night
If I take a drink is that against the law
And if I have a good time do you call that an act of war?

Well you better believe it boy this house is your home
I didn't build it up for you to live here on my own
And if you think it's easy to forget about me
You'd better think twice, you'd better believe
It's an act of war

We're living on the front line you and me
Fighting on this battleground of misery
Oh go ahead bring on your artillery
And we'll make this an act of war
Give it all you've got 'cause I'm all dug in
Keep the punches comin' I can take them on the chin
Winner takes all let the best man win
And we can call it an act of war
We can call it an act of war

Well I'm a man of convenience, I work a long hard day
After twelve long hours ain't I got the right to play
If living together is getting in the way
Then I call that an act of war

Well if that's your game then honey two can play
I'm going on the town tonight and have some fun my way
Ain't no way baby this girl's gonna stay
I call it an act of war

We're living on the front line you and me
Fighting on this battleground of misery
Oh go ahead bring on your artillery
And we'll make this an act of war
Give it all you've got 'cause I'm all dug in
Keep the punches comin' I can take them on the chin
Winner takes all let the best man win
And we can call it an act of war
And it looks like time
Ain't been on our side
If we could turn the clock back
We might survive
This act of war

a dandelion dies in the wind

See my eyes and I'll see your heart
The seagulls say you've gone
It was just a game of let's pretend
And I'll whistle to the waves that lend me tears
Purple clouds, golden rain, yesterday's gone
And a dandelion dies in the wind

If you're quick enough to rise
With the sleep still in your eyes
You will see the shadow of the sun above my mind
I know that only you can help me now
Purple clouds, golden rain, yesterday's gone
And a dandelion dies in the wind

But a dandelion sighs
When it tries to tell the wind
Cryin's not a bad thing
And worrying no sin
If they sent a cloud I would ride into the sky
To escape all of my troubles and to cast away your lies
Purple rain has turned to gold the clouds of yesterday
And the dandelion dies in the wind

all across the havens

The sister of sunlight
Comes to my lonely life,
Bearing the crosses I hung –
I hung on my lonely wife.

And the anchor told me,
If I prayed by the river,
That the sweet sound of water
Would always go with her.

All across the havens
To the waterfall,
They told me I would meet her there
Inside those icy walls.

But how on earth
In this universe
Can they forgive me of my pains,
For all across the Havens
I must stumble,
Locked in chains.

Then the mother of mercy
Showed me her stable,
And told me you would be safe,
Safe in her cradle.

And the waterfall opened,
And the water withdrew,
Leaving me standing
On a road leading through.

all quiet on the western front

All quiet on the Western Front, nobody saw
A youth asleep in the foreign soil, planted by the war.
Feel the pulse of human blood, pouring forth.
See the stems of Europe bend, under force.
All quiet, all quiet, all quiet on the Western front.

So tired of this garden's grief. Nobody cares.
Old kin kiss the small white cross, their only souvenir.
See the Prussian offence fly. Weren't we grand
To place the feel of cold sharp steel in their hands?
All quiet, all quiet, all quiet on the Western front.

It's gone all quiet on the Western front. Male angels sigh.
Ghosts float in a flooded trench, as Germany dies.
Fever reaps the flowers of France. Fair-haired boys
String the harps to Victory's voice, joyous noise.
All quiet, all quiet, all quiet on the Western front.

all the nasties

If it came to pass
That they should ask
What could I tell them?
Would they criticize
Behind my back,
Maybe I should let them.
Oh, if only then, and only then
They would understand.
They'd turn
A full-blooded city boy
Into a full-blooded city man.

If they could face it,
I could take it.
In their eyes
I know I'd make it.
Their tiny minds
And sacred cows, just fake it,
If only then, and only then
They would understand.
They'd turn
A full-blooded city boy
Into a full-blooded city man.

But I know the way
They want me,
In the way they publicize.
If they could turn
Their focus off,
To the image in their eyes.
Maybe it would help them –
Help them understand,
That a full-blooded city boy,
Is now a full-blooded city man.

all the girls love alice

Raised to be a lady by the golden rule,
Alice was the spawn of a public school.
With a double-barrelled name in the back of her brain,
And a simple case of 'Mummy doesn't love me' blues.

Reality it seems, was just a dream.
She couldn't get it on with the boys on the scene,
But what do you expect from a chick who's just sixteen?
And hey, hey, hey, you know what I mean.

All the young girls love Alice,
Tender young Alice they say,
Come over and see me
Come over and please me
Alice it's my turn today.

All the young girls love Alice,
Tender young Alice they say,
If I give you my number
Will you promise to call me
Wait till my husband's away.

Poor little darling with a chip out of her heart,
It's like acting in a movie when you've got the wrong part,
Getting your kicks in another girl's bed
And it was only last Tuesday they found you in the subway dead.

And who could you call your friends down in Soho?
One or two middle-aged dykes in a go-go
And what do you expect from a sixteen-year-old yo-yo?
And hey, hey, hey, oh don't you know.

amazes me

You're a cool little one
My dark southern breeze
Sweeps through my fingers
And it amazes me

Dixie shadowland
Your envy shelters me
Lay down your burden
Mystery of ebony

And it amazes me
Oh! it amazes me
Maybe the heat babe
Could be this tune
It amazes me
It amazes me
What drives me crazy
Is that big fat yellow moon

Look up that pale light
Well she's waking the trees
I'm drifting in your hoodoo
And it amazes me

Ain't no magic potion
No gri-gri on her side
She's bound to may salvation
Sweet little mama
Take me down by the river tonight
And It amazes me

amoreena

Lately I've been thinking how much I miss my lady
Amoreena's in the cornfield brightening the daybreak
Living like a lusty flower, running through the grass for hours
Rolling through the hay like a puppy child

And when it rains, the rain falls down
Washing out the cattle town
And she's far away somewhere in her eiderdown
And she dreams of crystal streams
Of days gone by when we would lean,
Laughing fit to burst upon each other

I can see you sitting eating apples in the evening
The fruit juice flowing slowly, slowly, slowly
Down the bronze of your body
Living like a lusty flower, running through the grass for hours
Rolling through the hay like a puppy child

Oh if only I could nestle in the cradle of your cabin
My arms around your shoulders the windows wide and open
While the swallow and the sycamore are playing in the valley
I miss you Amoreena like a king bee misses honey.

amy

Tread on my face if you like, little lady,
Turn me inside out if you have to baby,
But don't you cross me off your list.
I am young and I ain't never been kissed,
Never been kissed, by a lady called Amy.

You're far out, you're fab and insane,
A woman of the world it's quite plain.
My dad told me Amy's your name,
Said he'd break my neck if I played your game,
But he can bust my neck, 'cause I love you all the same.

Amy, I know you don't have to show your affection,
'Cause the big boys like you, and to you I'm an infection.
So if you don't want me around,
I think I'll run along and drown,
You can't want this bum in town, Amy.

I'm beaten on the streets 'cause I loves you,
I watch you go to work in the summer,
I don't whistle at you down the street
I would if I could, but I can't whistle you see.

Amy, I may not be James Dean,
Amy, I may not be nineteen,
And I may still be in romper boots and jeans,
But Amy, you're the girl that wrecks my dreams.

angeline

Well I'm work-shy, I'm wild-eyed
So shut that door when the baby cries
And keep me well fed, gimme warm bread
Lay my body on a feather bed

And spoil me, Angeline
Get to work
When the whistle screams Angeline
Maybe someday, someway
Somewhere in the future
There's more pay

Give me more cash, bring me sour mash
Peel me a grape and fetch my stash
And bite me, Angeline
Let me use you
Like a sex machine Angeline

You've got to swing that hammer
Punch that card
Angeline I love you
When you work so hard
Swing that hammer
And sew my jeans
Angeline just loves it
When I treat her mean

Well I talk tough, I act rough
Lay still honey
I can't get enough
And keep your nose clean
Let me be
On your knees
When you speak to me
And trust me, Angeline
And talk real dirty
And I'll make you scream Angeline

You've got to swing that hammer
Punch that card
Angeline I love you
When you work so hard
Swing that hammer
And sew my jeans
Angeline just loves it
When I treat her mean

a word in spanish

I don't know why,
I just know I do
I just can't explain
In this language that I use.
Something leaves me speechless
Each time that you approach
Each time you glide right through me
As if I was a ghost.

If I only could tell you
If you only would listen
I've got a line or two to use on you
I've got a romance we could christen.

There's a word in Spanish
I don't understand
But I heard it in a film one time
Spoken by the leading man
He said it with devotion
He sounded so sincere
And the words he spoke in Spanish
Brought the female lead to tears.
A word in Spanish, a word in Spanish.

If you can't comprehend.
Read it in my eyes
If you don't understand it's love
In a thin disguise
And what it takes to move you
Each time that you resist
Is more than just a pretty face
To prove that I exist.

If I only could tell you
If you only would listen
I've got a line or two to use on you
I've got a romance we could christen.

And there's a word in Spanish
I don't understand
But I heard it in a film one time
Spoken by the leading man
He said it with devotion
He sounded so sincere
And the words he spoke in Spanish
Brought the female lead to tears
A word in Spanish, a word in Spanish.

When manners make no difference
And my gifts all lay undone
I trade my accent in on chance
And fall back on a foreign tongue.

There's a word in Spanish
I don't understand
But I heard it in a film one time
Spoken by the leading man
He said it with devotion
He sounded so sincere
And the words he spoke in Spanish
Brought the female lead to tears.

bad side of the moon

It seems as though I've lived my life
On the bad side of the moon
To stir your dregs in sickness still
Without the rustic spoon.

Common people live with me
Where the light has never shone
And the hermits flock like hummingbirds
To speak in a foreign tongue.

I'm a light year away
From the people who make me stay
Sitting on the bad side of the moon.

There ain't no use for watchdogs here
To justify our ways,
We live our lives in manacles
The main cause of our stay.

Exiled here from other worlds
Our sentence comes too soon;
Why should I be made to pay
On the bad side of the moon?

ballad of a well-known gun

I pulled out my Stage Coach Times
And I read the latest news
I tapped my feet in dumb surprise
And of course I saw they knew
The Pinkertons they pulled out my bags
And asked me for my name
I stuttered out my answer and hung
My head in shame

Now they've found me,
At last they've found me
It's hard to run
From a starving family
Now they've found me,
I won't run
I'm tired of hearing,
There goes a well-known gun

Now I've seen this chain gang,
Let me see my priest
I couldn't have faced your desert sand,
Old burning brown-backed beast
The poor house they hit me for my kin,
And claimed my crumbling walls
Now I know how Reno felt,
When he ran from the law.

belfast

Deep inside
My soul fights a war
I can't explain
I can't cross over any more
All I see are dirty faces
Rain and wire
And common sense in pieces
But I try to see through Irish eyes,
Belfast

Look outside
Summer's lost and gone
It's a long walk
On a street of right and wrong
In every inch of sadness
Rocks and tanks
Go hand in hand with madness
But I never saw a braver place,
Belfast

And it's sad when they sing
And hollow ears listen
Of smoking black roses
On the streets of Belfast
And so say your lovers
From under the flowers
Every foot of this world
Needs an inch of Belfast

Who's to say
On whom Heaven smiles
Our different ways
We try hard to recognize
No more enchanted evenings
The pubs are closed
And all the ghosts are leaving
But you'll never let them shut you down,
Belfast

And it's sad when they sing
And hollow ears listen
Of smoking black roses
On the streets of Belfast
And so say your lovers
From under the flowers
Every foot of this world
Needs an inch of Belfast

The enemy is not at home
A jealous green
Streaks down this faulty diamond
No bloody boots or crucifix
Can ever hope to split this emerald island
But I never saw a braver place,
Belfast

believe

I believe in love
It's all we've got
Love has no boundaries
Costs nothing to touch
War makes money
Cancer sleeps
Curled up in my father
And that means something to me
Churches and dictators
Politics and papers
Everything crumbles
Sooner or later
But in love

I believe in love
It's all we've got
Love has no boundaries
No borders to cross
Love is simple
Hate breeds
Those who think difference
Is the child of disease
Fathers and son
Make love and guns
Families together
Kill someone
Without love

Without love
I wouldn't believe
In anything
That lives and breathes

Without love
I'd have no anger
I wouldn't believe
In the right to stand here
Without love
I wouldn't believe
I couldn't believe in you
And I wouldn't believe in me
Without love

I believe in love

bennie and the jets

Hey kids, shake it loose together,
The spotlight's hitting something
That's been known to change the weather.
We'll kill the fatted calf tonight
So stick around,
You're gonna hear electric music,
Solid walls of sound.

Say, Candy and Ronnie, have you seen them yet
But they're so spaced out, Bennie and the Jets,
But they're weird and they're wonderful,
Oh, Bennie she's really keen
She's got electric boots and mohair suits,
You know I read it in a magazine,
Oh! Bennie and the Jets.

Hey kids, plug into the faithless,
Maybe they're blinded
But Bennie makes them ageless.
We shall survive, let us take ourselves along,
Where we fight our parents out in the streets
To find who's right and who's wrong.

better off dead

There was a face on a hoarding
That someone had drawn on,
And just enough time for the night to pass by without warning.
Away in the distance there's a blue flashing light
Someone's in trouble somewhere tonight.
As the flickering neon stands ready to fuse
The wind blows away all of yesterday's news.

Well they've locked up their daughters
And battened the hatches.
They always could find us but they never could catch us.
Through the grease streaked window
Of an all-night cafe
We watched the arrested get taken away.
And that cigarette haze has ecology beat
As the whores and the drunks filed in from the street.

'Cause the steam's in the boiler the coal's in the fire
If you ask how I am then I'll just say inspired.
If the thorn of a rose is the thorn in your side
Then you're better off dead if you haven't yet died.

between seventeen and twenty

I wonder who's sleeping in your sheets tonight,
Whose head rests upon the bed
Could it be a close friend I knew so well.
Who seems to be so close to you instead, so close to you instead.

I'm blue tonight, I'm red when I'm mad.
I'm green when I'm jealous, yellow when I'm sad,
I guess I can't have everything,
So much has flown between the years when
I was twenty oh and you were seventeen.

And if I shower around three a.m.
It's just to wash away
The trace of a love unwanted
Oh in the times I went astray,
The times I went astray.

So out of choice I chose rock 'n' roll
But it pushed me to the limit everyday,
It turned me into a gypsy, kept me away from home
From there on, there seemed no use for you
For you to stay.

billie and the kids

Nothing looks as bad
After staying up all night
And the cruel words that cut you down
I never meant to write
And what came out as anger
Was lack of self control
Oh Billie won't you hold me
Once before you go

So leave me now
Don't turn around
It's the best thing you ever did
But it's hard for me to say goodbye
To Billie and the kids

Clever lies keep coming
Some men never change
I'm a hand that's raised in anger
The blow that causes pain
And I just can't be trusted
With a bottle and a child
Oh Billie it's no wonder
You say I've never tried

billy bones and the white bird

Take the wheel I hear the timbers creaking
Take the wheel I think this ship is sinking
Jamaica suns so far and I've been thinking
Old Billy Bones has gone to sea
And quit his dockside drinking.

Check it out, check it out, check it out.

And when I'm dead who'll fly the White Bird home
I'm not the ancient mariner your children know.
And the sea's the field these old jack tars have sown
'Cause Billy Bones just wants to know
Who'll fly the White Bird home.

Check it out, check it out, check it out.

Your majesty, your majesty
I heard the bosun cry
Old Billy Bones has washed ashore
Upon a foreign tide.

bite your lip
(get up and dance!)

She slid down to the city limits
Monkey time in fifteen minutes
Bite your lip, get up, get up and dance.
Don't let me down
Please stick around
Bite your lip, get up, get up and dance.

Strobe light on funky feet,
Soul children in the disco heat.
Top dog, top cat,
Move that muscle and shake that fat.
Bite your lip, get up, get up and dance.

Chicago, L.A.
Everyplace, everyway
Bite your lip, get up, get up and dance.

Illinois, Santa Fe,
Do do do do do do do what I say.
Bite your lip, get up, get up and dance.

bitter fingers

'I'm going on the circuit
I'm doing all the clubs,
And I really need a song boys
To stir those workers up,
And get their wives to sing it with me
Just like in the pubs.
When I worked the good old pubs in Stepney.'

'Oh could you knock a line or two
Together for a friend?
Sentimental, tear inducing with a happy end.
And we need a tune to open
Our summer season at Southend.
Can you help us?'

It's hard to write a song with bitter fingers,
So much to prove, so few to tell you why,
Those old die-hards in Denmark Street start laughing
At the keyboard player's hollow haunted eyes.
It seems to me a change is really needed
I'm sick of tra la las and la de das.
No more long days hocking hunks of garbage
Bitter fingers never swung on swinging stars.

I like the warm blue flame
The hazy heat it brings,
It loosens up the muscles
And forces you to sing.
You know it's just another hit and run
From the tin pan alley twins.

'And there's a chance that one day
You might write a standard lads.
So churn 'em out thick and fast
And we'll still pat your backs.
Cause we need what we can get
To launch another dozen acts.
Are you working?'

blessed

Hey you, you're a child in my head
You haven't walked yet
Your first words have yet to be said
But I swear you'll be blessed

I know you're still just a dream
Your eyes might be green
Or the bluest that I've ever seen
Anyway you'll be blessed

And you, you'll be blessed
You'll have the best
I promise you that
I'll pick a star from the sky
Pull your name from a hat
I promise you that
I promise you that
Promise you that
You'll be blessed

I need you before I'm too old
To have and to hold
To walk with you and watch you grow
And know that you're blessed

And you, you'll be blessed
You'll have the best
I promise you that
i'll pick a star from the sky
Pull your name from a hat
I promise you that
Promise you that you,

You'll be blessed
You'll have the best
I promise you that
I'll pick a star from the sky
Pull your name from a hat
I promise you that
I promise you that
Promise you that
You'll be blessed

I promise you that
You'll be blessed
Promise you that
You'll be blessed
Promise you that
You'll be blessed

blue avenue

I gotta quit this habit
It's like some drug for you
You've been my sweet sweet addict
I've been your little white boy blue

You've got the same obsession
We ain't no cat and mouse
You linger on my lips like confession
You laid the traps in this house

And it's no use, each way we lose
You and me at the crossroad of Blue Avenue
Hit and run hearts collide here
True love passes through
Looks like we've got a wreck babe
Up on Blue Avenue
Up on Blue Avenue
Blue Avenue

Two hearts get entangled
Dirty minds they go to town
Everyone's got an angle
Little lies get spread around

Let them say what they want
You and me we already knew
Takes more than hocus pocus babe
To save you from Blue Avenue

blues for my baby and me

Your old man got mad, when I told him we were leaving.
He cursed and he raged and he swore at the ceiling.
He called you his child, said honey get wise to his game.
He'll get you in trouble, I know it, those bums are all the same.
There's a greyhound outside in the lane, it's waiting for us,
So tell him Goodbye, we gotta go west on that bus.

And it's all over now,
Don't you worry no more,
Gonna go west to the sea,
The greyhound is swaying,
And the radio's playing,
Some blues for baby and me,
And the highway looks like it never did,
Lord, it looks so sweet and so free,
And I can't forget that trip to the west,
Singing blues for baby and me.

Saw your hands trembling, your eyes opened in surprise,
It's ninety in the shade, babe, and there ain't a cloud in the sky.
I called you my child, said honey, now this is our game,
There's two of us to play it and I'm happy to be home again.
There's a greyhound outside in the lane, it's waiting for us
So tell him goodbye, We gotta go west on that bus.

boogie pilgrim

Crime in the streets
I read about it every day in the papers
Justice needs and Justice wants
But just in time's too late here.
Oh, feels like I wasn't born there
I feel just like a Boogie Pilgrim.

Boogie Pilgrim
Hustled to get it
To get it together
Boogie Pilgrim, oh
Brother I never felt better.

Low life's complete
When you've lived that way out on the sidewalk
Oh I got the speed if you got the need
But the need in me needs nothing
But I know that you all want something
Oh, just like Boogie Pilgrim.

border song

Holy Moses, I have been removed,
I have seen the spectre, he has been here too,
Distant cousin from down the line
Brand of people who ain't my kind
Holy Moses, I have been removed

Holy Moses, I have been deceived,
Now the wind has changed direction and I'll have to leave
Won't you please excuse my frankness but it's not my cup of tea
Holy Moses, I have been deceived

I'm going back to the border
Where my affairs, my affairs ain't abused.
I can't take any more bad water
I've been poisoned from my head down to my shoes

Holy Moses I have been deceived.

Holy Moses, let us live in peace
Let us strive to find a way to make all hatred cease
There's a man over there, what's his colour I don't care
He's my brother let us live in peace

breaking hearts (ain't what it used to be)

They used to say that boys are tough as nails
In everyway he keeps his heart as guarded as a jail
Now things have changed, I feel so old
Like any girl could drag my heart across the coals

I was always there in the thick of things
I always had the heart of every woman on a string
The danger zone shone from my eyes
I seemed like every inch I gained became a mile

It's not the night, reaching in and touching me
It's just that breaking hearts ain't what it used to be
It seems that time has killed that cruel streak in me
And breaking hearts ain't what it used to be

It's not the light shining in and catching me
It's just that breaking hearts ain't what it used to be
But time has come and cast a spell on me
And breaking hearts ain't what it used to be

And now I know what lonely means
I used to give so little and gain everything
The darkest part of everyday
Is the shadow of another girl as she turn and walks away
Can't say I blame them all for being hurt
After all I treated each and everyone like dirt
Who wants a heart that's never home
I face the facts and lock myself into a life alone

burn down the mission

You tell me there's an angel in your tree
Did he say he'd come to call on me
For things are getting desperate in our home
Living in the parish of the restless folks I know

Bring your family down to the riverside
Look to the east to see where the fat stock hide
Behind four walls of stone the rich man sleeps
It's time we put the flame torch to their keep

Burn down the mission
If we're gonna stay alive
Watch the black smoke fly to heaven
See the red flame light the sky

Burn down the mission
Burn it down to stay alive
It's our only chance of living
Take all you need to live inside

Deep in the woods the squirrels are out today
My wife cried when they came to take me away
But what more could I do just to keep her warm
Than burn, burn, burn, burn down the mission walls.

burning buildings

It used to be a sweet sensation
No price too high for love
Now I pay for this bitter taste
And the price is not enough
Such cruel sport for your kicks
Such hard knocks on my heart
How long before the pain ends
Tell me where living starts

And lovers leap off burning buildings
Waking up on a sky high wire
Desperation leaves us clinging
On the edge of a house on fire

Lovers leap off burning buildings
Live our life on borrowed time
Every flame that ever moved you
Touched your lips but never mine

No room for conversation
Cold stares and angry words
Fall in pieces from our faces
We read do not disturb
Some lovers just go hungry
Others beg for just a bite
You use me under pressure
To whet your appetite

cage the songbird

Sober in the morning light
Things look so much different
To how they looked last night.
A pale face pressed to an unmade bed
Like flags of many nations flying high above her head.

The cellophane still on the flowers
The telegram still in her hand
As whispers circulate all day
Their back-stage baby princess passed away.

And you can cage the songbird
But you can't make her sing,
And you can trap the free bird,
But you'll have to clip her wings,
'Cause she'll soar like a hawk when she flies
But she'll dive like an eagle when she dies.

Promises of no more lies,
Fell flat upon an empty stage
Before the audience arrived.
A return in time to the cheaper seats
She never knew what lay beneath
Just a dated handbill they found between the sheets.

Let down before the final curtain
A shallow heart that left her cold.
She left in rouge upon the mirror
A circled kiss to the faithful fans who'd miss her.

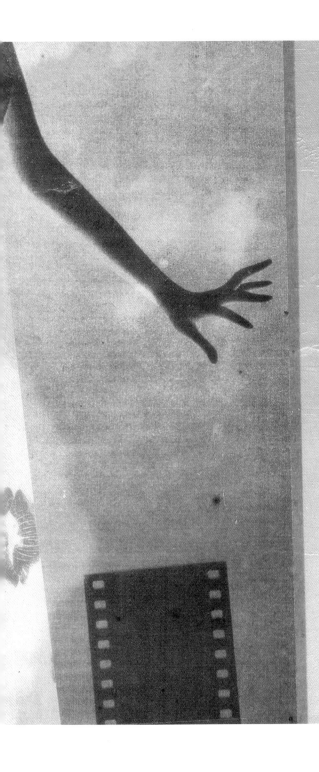

candle in the wind

Goodbye Norma Jean,
Though I never knew you at all
You had the grace to hold yourself
While those around you crawled,
They crawled out of the woodwork,
And they whispered into your brain,
They set you on the treadmill
And they made you change your name.

And it seems to me you lived your life
Like a candle in the wind,
Never knowing who to cling to
When the rain set in.
And I would have liked to have known you
But I was just a kid.
Your candle burned out long before
Your legend ever did.

Loneliness was tough,
The toughest role you ever played.
Hollywood created a superstar
And pain was the price you paid.
Even when you died
The press still hounded you —
All the papers had to say
Was that Marilyn was found in the nude.

Goodbye Norma Jean,
Though I never knew you at all
You had the grace to hold yourself
While those around you crawled.

Goodbye Norma Jean,
From the young man in the twenty-second row
Who sees you as something more than sexual,
More than just our Marilyn Monroe.

candy by the pound

Well I'm keepin' off the streets since you came to town
Since you claimed my heart from the lost and found
I've said goodbye to my foolin' round
Now you and me babe we got candy by the pound

Well I never knew it could feel so good
Be the king of the hill in my neighbourhood
Rain on my roof what a sweet sound
Oh with you underneath it's like candy by the pound

You can tell everybody that this girl of mine
Is sweeter than the grapes hanging from the vine
Love like wine honey drinkin' till I drown
Keep it comin' baby like candy by the pound

Oh no what's come over me
If I am dreamin' then let me sleep
Oh wow I'm heaven bound
Love is getting sweeter than candy by the pound

Now I'm ducking in the alley out of common sense
Hidin' from the claws of my old girlfriend
She's screamin' murder beatin' my door down
While I'm right behind it eatin' candy by the pound
I'm right behind it eatin' candy by the pound

can I put you on

I work in the foundry for a penny and a half a day,
Like a blind street-musician I never see those who pay.
It's dirty work in Birmingham,
Better deal for a Sheffield man,
If he can rivet, then his kids can buy
Candy from the candy man.

And the van that comes round weekends
Selling fancy city things,
Sold by the man in the trilby hat
And whiskers spread like wings.
You can hear him sing,
Oh, you can hear him sing –
Can I put you on? People, can I put you on?
Tell you that I love you, people,
Sing a salesman's song,
And put you on.

And a second cousin works in the pits in Newcastle upon Tyne,
And he don't care if it rains outside, there's coal-dust on his mind.
It's dirty work in Manchester,
But the crew gets paid its gelt
Bang on the bell on Friday,
You buys a little something for yourself.

captain fantastic and
the brown dirt cowboy

Captain Fantastic, raised and regimented
Hardly a hero,
Just someone his mother might know,
Very clearly a case for corn flakes and classics,
'Two teas both with sugar please.'
In the back of an alley.
While little Dirt Cowboys turned brown in their saddles
Sweet chocolate biscuits,
And red rosy apples in summer.
For it's hay make
And 'Hey mom, do the papers say anything good.
Are there chances in life for little Dirt Cowboys,
Should I make my way out of my home in the woods?'

Brown Dirt Cowboy
Still green and growing.
City slick Captain,
Fantastic the feedback
The honey the hive could be holding.
For there's weak winged young sparrows
That starve in the winter,
Broken young children
On the wheels of the winners.
And the sixty-eight summer festival wallflowers
And thinning.

For cheap easy meals
Are hardly a home on the range.
Too hot for the band
With a desperate desire for change.
We've thrown in the towel too many times
Out for the count when we're down.
Captain Fantastic and the Brown Dirt Cowboy
From the end of the world to your town.

And all this talk of Jesus
Coming back to see us
Couldn't fool us.
For we were spinning out our lines
Walking on the wire,
Hand in hand went music and the rhyme.
The Captain and the Kid
Stepping in the ring,
From here on sonny
It's a long and lonely climb.

cartier

If your life is dull and dreary,
And you're feeling rather weary,
Of the mundane things that clutter up one's life
Drive your roller up to Bond Street
Where royalty and sheiks meet
Make your day
Here's the thing to do
Spend a grand or two at Cartier

chameleon

The last I heard of you,
You were somewhere on a cruise in the Mediterranean.
So, imagine my surprise to see you very much alive
In the English rain again.

And I can still recall wet afternoons,
When we were small and simply childish.
But you've created your own ghost
And the need you have is more than most to hide it.

Oh, Chameleon, you're stealing your way back into my eyes,
Beyond a shadow of a doubt, you're a devil, you're a devil in disguise.
Do you really change me, or am I going crazy?
Chameleon, Chameleon, Chameleon, you're free again my child.

I remember still those lazy summer days we'd kill out hunting danger,
And we were alien to all outsiders
We had no desire to talk to strangers.

chasing the crown

I built a wall in China, I sank an ocean liner
I've wrecked homes, I've burned thrones, chasing the crown.
I've put the thorns in your feet, I spread plague in the streets
I've sprung traps, confused maps, chasing the crown

Chasing the crown till he bites the apple
I was lickin' my lips till his Son come down –
I'm chasing the crown, the crown, I'm chasing the crown
I'm taking a turn in the right direction
By leaving his soul in the lost and found
Chasing the crown, I'm chasing the crown.

I saw the tea float in Boston, I saw the live wire shock 'em
I made them float, I made them drown, chasing the crown
I laid the desert sands, I froze the polar caps
Well, they'd dry out, and I'd shout Hey I'm chasing the crown.

club at the end of the street

When the shades are drawn
And the light of the moon is banned
And the stars up above
Walk the heavens hand in hand
There's a shady place
At the end of the working day
Where young lovers go
And this hot little trio plays

That's where we meet
That's where we meet
Me and you rendezvous
In the club at the end of the street

Ooh where we meet
Ooh where we meet
Me and you rendezvous
In the club at the end of the street

From the alleyways
Where the catwalks gently sway
You hear the sound of Otis
And the voice of Marvin Gaye
In this smokey room
There's a jukebox plays all night
And we can dance real close
Beneath the pulse of a neon light

That's where we meet
Me and you rendezvous
In the club at the end of the street
Ooh where we meet
Ooh where we meet
Me and you rendezvous
In the club at the end of the street

There's a downtown smell of cooking
From the flame on an open grill
There's a sax and a big bass pumpin'
Lord have mercy
Ooh, ya can't sit still

cold

You don't love him any more
He threw your rag doll out the door
I kept my distance, I held my breath
Love always ends up
Hanging by a thread

Love hurts so much
Love leaves a scar
'I don't love you' is like a stake
Being driven through your heart

But I don't care
I came back for you
Love is cruel, but I don't care
I wanted you
And I'm cold, cold, cold

You said don't cry to me
He said I'm a dead man if you leave
I have no feelings, I have no heart
Love always cuts out
The warm and tender part

Love hurts so much
Love cuts so deep
It's a hot sweat and a cold shake
Like drowning in your sleep

But I don't care
I came back for you
Love is cruel, but I don't care
I wanted you
And I'm cold, cold, cold

Love hurts so much
Love leaves a scar
'I don't love you' is like a stake
Being driven through your heart

But I don't care
I came back for you
I don't care

I came back for you
Love is cruel, but I don't care
I wanted you
And I'm cold, cold, cold

cold as christmas

We still sit at separate tables
And we sleep at different times
And the warm wind in the palm trees
Hasn't helped to change our minds
It was the lure of the tropics
That I thought might heal the scars
Of a love burned out by silence
In a marriage minus heart

And I call the kids on the telephone
Say there's something wrong out here
It's July but it's cold as Christmas
In the middle of the year
The temperature's up to ninety-five
But there's a winter look
In your mother's eyes
And to melt the tears
There's a heatwave here
So how come it's as cold as Christmas
In the middle of the year

I dreamed of love
In a better climate
And for what it's really worth
I put faith in the star we followed
To this Caribbean surf
But there's an icy fringe
On everything
And I cannot find the lines
Where's the beauty
In the beast we made
Why the frost in the summertime

cold highway

Your life stepped lightly out our hands,
When no one's looking out you understand,
Your world was a wheel but the cog ceased to turn,
The bottom fell out and our fingers got burned.

And there's a cold, cold highway,
That the wind whistles down,
Where the corners turn blind,
Like the graveyard ground,
Oh your black icy snare,
Once cut down my friend,
In the deepest dark winter,
When the world seemed to end.

Every new version of the way of life,
Leaves you reckless and searching for stars in the night,
But whose kid are you when they finally decide?
The lifestyle you led and the way that you died.

But they're oh so simple,
They're oh so simple,
They're still trying to tell,
The difference for you between heaven and hell,
They're trying to find something,
Your legends are found,
But all they bought you was a hole in the ground.

Years rolling by just like a dream,
I'm partly human and I'm partly machine,
They've lost you and fate put your name on a stone,
Perhaps now, my friend, they might leave you alone.

32

come down in time

In the quiet silent seconds I turned off the light switch
And I came down to meet you in the half light the moon left
While a cluster of night jars sang some songs out of tune
A mantle of bright light shone down from a room

Come down in time I still hear her say
So clear in my ear like it was today
Come down in time was the message she gave
Come down in time and I'll meet you half way

Well I don't know if I should have heard her as yet
But a true love like hers is a hard love to get
And I've walked most all the way and I ain't heard her call
And I'm getting to thinking if she's coming at all

Come down in time I still hear her say
So clear in my ear like it was today
Come down in time was the message she gave
Come down in time and I'll meet you half way

There are women and women, and some hold you high
While some leave you counting the stars in the night

country comfort

Soon the pines will be falling everywhere
Village children fight each other for a share
And the six-o-nine goes roaring past the creek
Deacon Lee prepares his sermon for next week

I saw grandma yesterday, down at the store
Well she's really going fine for eighty-four
Well she asked me if sometime I'd fix her barn
Poor old girl she needs a hand to run the farm

And it's good old country comfort in my bones
Just the sweetest sound my ears have ever known
Just an old-fashioned feeling fully-grown
Country comfort's any truck that's going home

Down at the well, they've got a new machine
Foreman says it cuts man-power by fifteen
But that ain't natural, well so old Clay would say
You see he's a horse-drawn man until his dying day

Now the old fat goose is flying cross the sticks
The hedgehog's done in clay between the bricks
And the rocking chair's a-creakin' on the porch
Across the valley moves the herdsman with his torch

crazy water

On a bench, on the beach
Just before the sun had gone,
I tried to reach you
Plain faced and falling fast
You looked so vacant, like an empty shell
Whose life had passed upon the ocean.

Before light shook the sky
Down by the docks I saw
The masts unfolding
Don't turn away, please understand
It's a life and a living
And a way to keep the wolves away
From hungry hands, from hungry hands.

Crazy water
Takes my fishing boat on Monday morning
Dangerous dreaming
If we all believe in the things you believe you're seeing
Oh we'd never drop our nets in the crazy water, crazy water.

Tangled lives, lonely wives
Shoreline widows pray
For the souls of missing whalers
Endless on an endless sea
Where nothing lives between us
Just the breakers on the ocean
Separating you and me

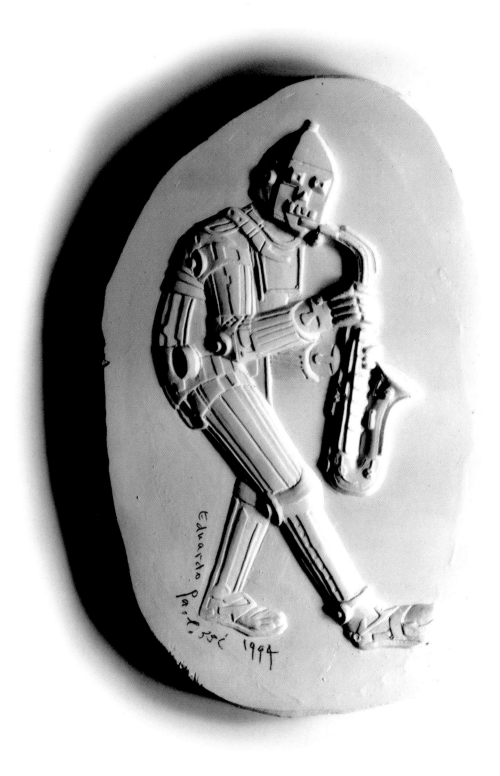

crocodile rock

I remember when rock was young
Me and Susie had so much fun,
Holding hands and skimmin' stones
Had an old gold Chevy and a place of my own.

But the biggest kick I ever got,
Was doing a thing called the Crocodile Rock,
While the other kids were rocking round the clock,
We were hoppin' and boppin' to the Crocodile Rock.

Well, Crocodile Rockin' is something shockin'
When your feet just can't keep still,
I never knew me a better time,
And I guess I never will.

Oh Lawdy mama those Friday nights,
When Susie wore her dresses tight,
And, the Crocodile Rockin' was out of sight.

But the years went by and rock just died,
Susie went and left me for some foreign guy,
Long nights cryin' by the record machine,
Dreamin' of my Chevy and my old blue jeans.

But they'll never kill the thrills we got,
Burning up to the Crocodile Rock,
Learning fast as the weeks went past,
We really thought the Crocodile Rock would last.

cry to heaven

I found a black beret
On the street today
It was lying in the gutter all torn
There's a white flag flying
On a tall building
But the kids just watch the storm

Their dirty faces
Pressed on the windows
Shattered glass before their eyes
There's a mad dog barking
In a burned out subway
Where the sniper sleeps at night

No birthday songs to sing again
Just bricks and stones to give them
Wrap them up in your father's flags
And let them cry to heaven

There are many graves
By a cold lake
As the beds were when your babies are born
And your rag doll sits
With a permanent grin
But the kids just watch the storm

I saw a black cat
Tease a white mouse
Until he killed it with his claws
Seems a lot of countries
Do the same thing
Before they go to war

crystal

We're caught up in a web you and I
Since Crystal came between us
The knots of friendship
Seem to be untied
And it hurts me most to cheat,
And that's no lie
She can swing us both forever
In the long run
She's the one who must decide

And if she leaves me,
Handle her with care
Don't hurt little Crystal
And if she calls you long distance,
Just be there
Oh Crystal
The world is your oyster,
You're a pearl
But he's a jewel, and my friend
I'm sure that in the end, Crystal,
You'll be his little girl
Oh Crystal

You're stronger than me but I'm sure
That the fight would fall to no one
The cold hard truth
Is stronger than us all
And it breaks my heart
To see us go this far
We're just captives
In our separate cells
And without her there's
No peace behind these bars

curtains

I used to know this old scarecrow
He was my song
My joy and sorrow,
Cast alone between the furrows
Of a field no longer sown by anyone.
I held a dandelion
That said the time had come
To leave upon the wind
Not to return,
When summer burned the earth again.

 Cultivate the freshest flower
This garden ever grew,
Beneath these branches
I once wrote such childish words for you.
But that's okay.
There's treasure children always seek to find,
And just like us
You must have had
A Once Upon A Time.

dancin' in
the end zone

Have you ever had a good time turn bad
When the leaves turn brown
And the shattered glass just splinters
It's days like this that you can't resist
A long tall drink
And a big yellow sun in the winter

And you can go dancin'
You can go dancin'
You can go dancin'
Dancin' in the end zone

Did you ever pray you could stay away
Company excluded
From the curse of the family circle
In a big round room on the edge of the moon
There's a shooting star
In a race for the final hurdle

And you can go dancin'
You can go dancin'
You can go dancin'
Dancin' in the end zone

No need to worry
No need to worry
No need to worry
When you dance alone
You already made it
You already made it
When you're dancin' in the end zone

And you can go dancin'
You can go dancin'
You can go dancin'
Dancin' in the end zone

38

dan dare
(pilot of the future)

Can you tell me how
Old Dan might have done it
If he'd been here now.
Holy cow My stars
Might have been mad on the planet Mars.
Because I don't have foresight to see
If we'll still be together
In the twenty-first
In the twenty-first century.
He's our flying ace
Pilot of the future
In an endless space.
Holy cow My eyes
Never saw a rocket that was quite tha size.
Because I don't have the energy
To be cat and mouse
For the champions –
For the champions of destiny.

So long Captain Dan
I fail to see what motivates your hands
Goodbye restless night
You know I loved Dan Dare
But I couldn't make his flight.
So long, so long
Dan Dare doesn't know it
He doesn't know it
He doesn't know
But I liked the Mekon.

daniel

Daniel is travelling tonight on a plane
I can see the red tail lights heading for Spain,
Oh and I can see Daniel waving goodbye,
God it looks like Daniel, must be the clouds in my eyes.

They say Spain is pretty, though I've never been,
Well Daniel says its the best place he's ever seen,
Oh and he should know he's been there enough,
Lord I miss Daniel, Oh I miss him so much.

Oh Daniel my brother,
You are older than me,
Do you still feel the pain
Of the scars that won't heal?
Your eyes have died, but you see more than I,
Daniel you're a star in the face of the sky.

did he shoot her

Sling your hook in with him baby
He's a real sharp-shooter now
If he's out there hiding in the tall grass
Tell him I said he was a coward

This ain't any old western honey
It's the twentieth century now
But if he thinks he's some kinda tough cowboy
And he's hurt her then I wanna know how

Did he shoot her
With his compromise
Like a heart attack
He can paralyse
Or did he hang her in a noose
On the telephone line?

Did he shoot her
With a 45?
Did he leave his mark
Right between her eyes
Oh did he shoot that girl
That used to be mine?

Tell him I'm ready any time he chooses
The pay-off for the things, for the things he's done
He ain't messin' with no two-bit bandit
Armed with a couple of guns

If he wants to see it as a two-reel movie
He's livin' in the head of someone else
But better take him down and dust him honey
I wanna hear the truth for myself

dirty little girl

I've seen a lot of women who haven't had much luck,
I've seen you looking like you've been run down by a truck.
That ain't nice to say, sometimes I guess I'm really hard,
But I'm gonna put buckshot in your pants if you step into my yard.

When I watch the police come by and move you on
Well I sometimes wonder what's beneath the mess you've become.
Well you may have been a pioneer in the trade of women's wear,
But all you got was a mop-up job, washing other people's stairs.

I'm gonna tell the world, you're a dirty little girl,
Someone grab that bitch by the ears.
Rub her down scrub her back
And turn her inside out,
'Cause I bet she hasn't had a bath in years.

Here's my own belief about all the dirty girls
That you have to clean the oyster to find the pearl.
And like rags that belong to you, I belong to myself,
So don't show up round here 'til your social worker's helped.

dixie lily

Showboat comin' up the river
See her lanterns flicker in the gentle breeze
I can hear the crickets singin' in the evening
Old Dixie Lily movin' past the cypress trees.

My little boat she rocks easy
I've been catchin' the catfish in the creek all day
Oh, and I've never seen ladies like those on the big boats
Must be fancy breedin' lets you live that way.

Dixie Lily, chuggin' like a grand old lady
Paddles hittin' home in the noonday sun
Ploughin' through the water with your whistles blowin'
Down from Louisiana on the Vicksburg run.

Papa says that I'm a dreamer
Says them skeetas bit me one too many times
Oh, but I never get lonesome living on the river
Watchin' old Lily leave the world behind.

don't go
breaking my heart

Don't go breaking my heart
I couldn't if I tried
Oh honey if I get restless
Baby you're not that kind.

Don't go breaking my heart
You take the weight off my mind
Oh honey when you knock on my door
Ooo I gave you my key.

OoOo nobody knows it
When I was down
I was your clown

OoOo nobody knows it
Right from the start
I gave you my heart
Oh oh. . . I gave you my heart.

So don't go breaking my heart
I won't go breaking your heart
Don't go breaking my heart.

And nobody told us
'Cause nobody showed us
And now it's up to us babe
Oh I think we can make it.

don't let the sun
go down on me

I can't light no more of your darkness
All my pictures seem to fade to black and white
I'm growing tired and time stands still before me
Frozen here on the ladder of my life.

Too late to save myself from falling
I took a chance and changed your way of life
But you misread my meaning when I met you
Closed the door and left me blinded by the light.

Don't let the sun go down on me
Although I search myself it's always someone else I see
I'd just allow a fragment of your life to wander free
But losing everything is like the sun going down on me.

I can't find Oh, the right romantic line
But see me once and see the way I feel
Don't discard me just because you think I mean you harm
But these cuts I have, Oh they need love to help them heal.

durban deep

I won't see you till Christmas
I breathe coal dust, I get blisters
But the foreman he don't worry
He say work boy there's no hurry
Don't that big red sun
Look a lot like fire
When you come out of the ground
After forty-eight hours

Goin' down, down, down, down, down
Goin' down in Durban deep
Goin' down, down, down, down, down
There's no mercy in my sleep
I just hear the drill an' hammer
Feel the killin' heat
Goin' two miles down to the heart
Of Durban deep.

I was born on amen corner
I pound rock face, I get lonely
But my family they go hungry
Still the boss man he call us lazy
Don't the ole blue heaven
Look a lot like your eyes
When you're blinded by the brightness
Of the Transvaal sky

Goin' down, down, down, down, down
Goin' down in Durban deep
Goin' down, down, down, down, down
There's no mercy in my sleep
I just hear the drill an' hammer
Feel the killin' heat
Goin' two miles down to the heart
Of Durban deep

easier to walk away

Everytime you turn around you
Wear another face
Everytime I look away I
Find a hiding place

If you knew me like you know him
You would know just how I feel
Slipping through somebody's fingers
Falling under someone's wheels

It's easier to walk away
Better off to face the fact
When love holds you up for ransom
Walk away and don't look back

Never seen you looking back through
Smiling eyes and tears
Never knew you holding on to
Memories and fears

Just release me I can't take it
Can't you see a change has come
Strangled by infatuation
Buried under someone's thumb

It's easier to walk away
Cover up and fade to black
When love scars and leaves you branded
Walk away and don't look back

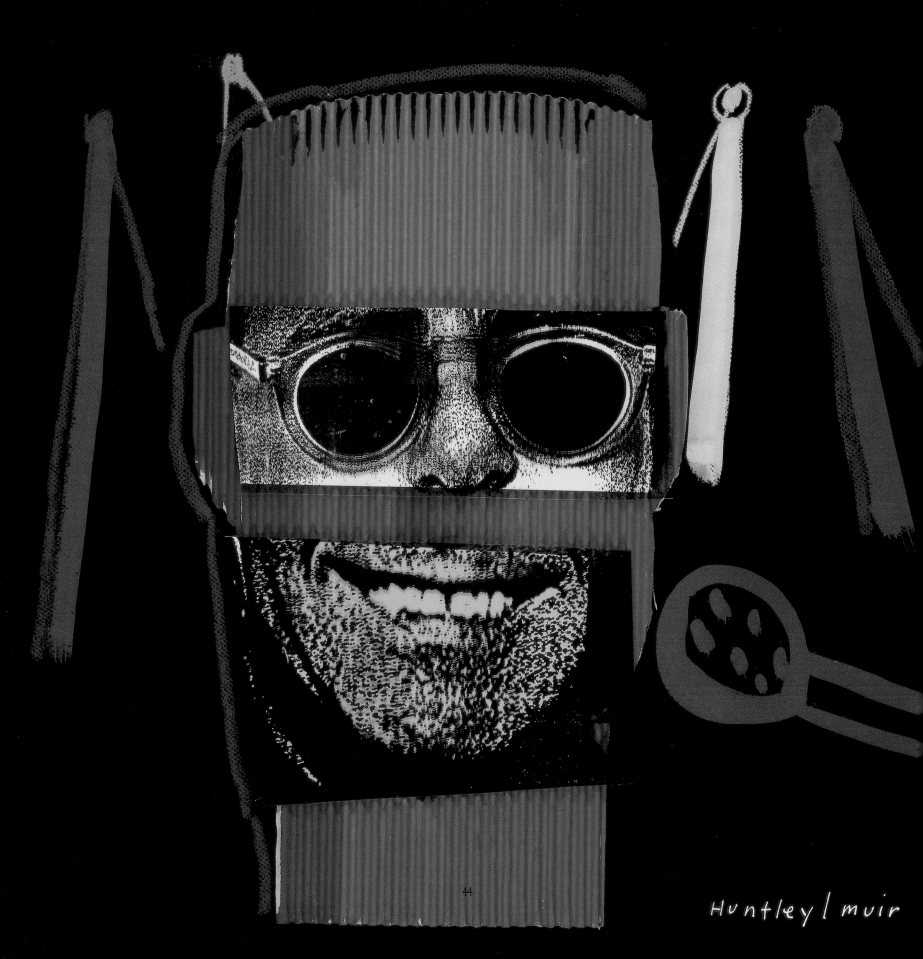

44

Huntley/muir

ego

Take a look at me now
Take a taste of the money
I'm not in it for the bread
I'm in it for the gravy, honey
Step in the thin ice lightly
And check out the show twice nightly
Oh, 'cause I'm on the stage tonight
And if the price is right,
I wear my face before the lights

I crave the lights
Blinding white
I need the lights, tonight
Take a look at me now
Take a look at my billing
I'm not in it as an extra
I'm in it for the killing
Inflate my egos gently, tell them heaven sent me
Oh, 'cause I'm so expressive
And I'm so obsessed with my ego, my ego

And it's nothing more
Inform the press
Invite the guests
I need the press, tonight

Do you remember acting out your youth
A romeo resplendent upon an orange crate
Do you remember how I would recite
And how I'd blow my lines and hide my face

Oh maybe I was childish, foolish, before school-ish,
Immature-ish, lose your cool-ish
I have to grow through my ego

Take a look at me now
Take a taste of the money
I'm not in it for the gravy, honey
Inflate my egos gently, tell them heaven sent me
Oh, 'cause I'm so expressive
And I'm so obsessed with my ego, my ego

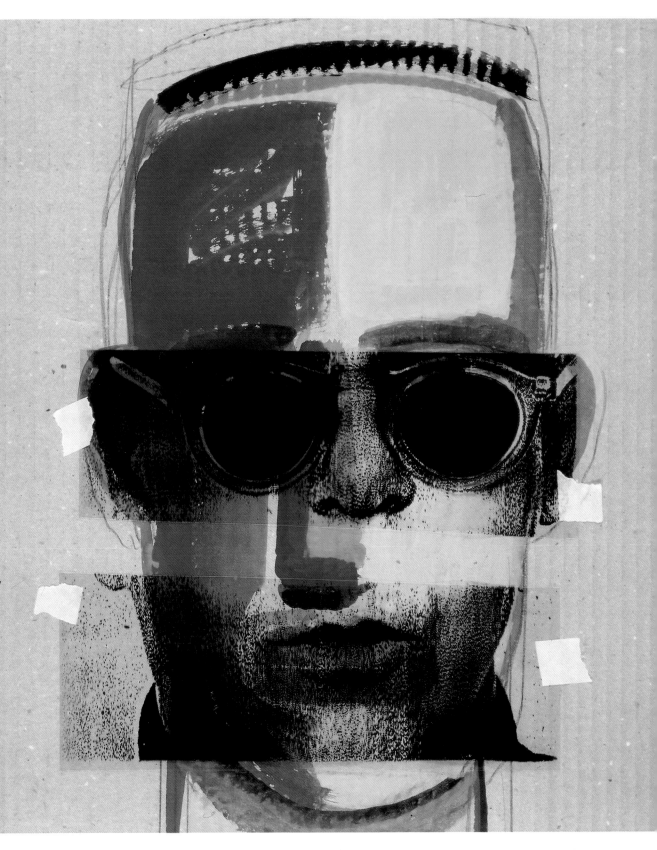

elderberry wine

There's a fly in the window, a dog in the yard,
And a year since I saw you,
There's a trunk in the corner, I keep all my letters,
My bills and demands I keep too.

But I can't help thinkin' about the times,
You were a wife of mine,
You aimed to please me, cooked blacked-eyed peas-me,
Made Elderberry Wine.

Drunk all the time, feelin' fine,
On Elderberry Wine,
Those were the days, we'd lay in the haze,
Forget depressive times.

How can I ever get it together,
Without a wife in line,
To pick the crop and get me hot,
On Elderberry Wine.

Round a tree in the summer, a fire in the fall,
Flat out when we couldn't stand,
The bottle went round, like a woman down South,
Passed on from hand to hand.

But I can't help thinkin' about the times,
You were a wife of mine,
You aimed to please me, cooked blacked-eyed peas-me,
Made Elderberry Wine.

emily

The church bells ring out morning glory
When summer bends to the winter's rage
Emily walks through the cemetery
Passed a dog in an unmarked grave
The old girl hobbles, nylons sagging
Talks to her sisters in the ground
'I saw a lie in the mirror this morning
I hear a prophecy all around.'

And Emily they come and go
The shadows and the distant sounds
But Emily don't be afraid
When the weight of angels weighs you down

Emily prays to a faded hero
In a little frame clutched to her gown
Hears the voice of promise in his memory
'Tonight's the night they let the ladder down'
In a cage sits a gold canary
By a wicker chair and a rosewood loom
As a soul ascends aboard the evening
Canary sings to an empty room

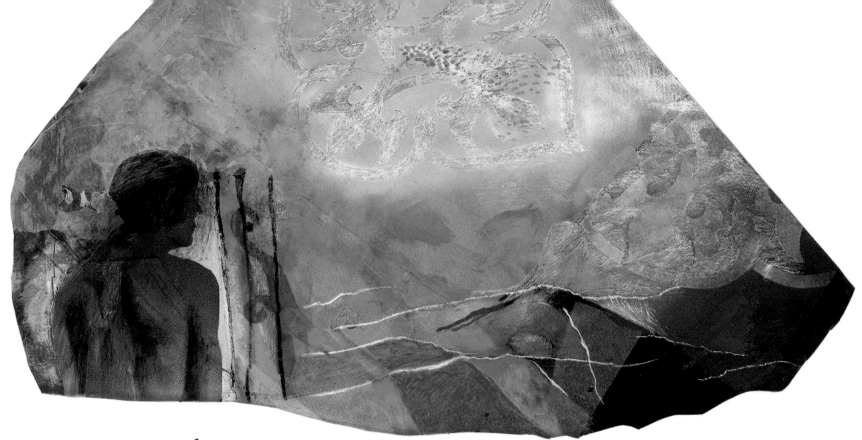

empty garden
(hey hey johnny)

What happened here?
As the New York sunset disappeared
I found an empty garden among the flagstones there
Who lived here?
He must have been a gardener that cared a lot
Who weeded out the tears and grew a good crop
But now it all looks strange, it's funny how one insect
Can damage so much grain

And what's it for?
This little empty garden by the brownstone door
And in the cracks along the sidewalk, nothing grows no more
Who lived here?
He must have been a gardener that cared a lot
Who weeded out the tears and grew a good crop
And we are so amazed, we're crippled and we're dazed
A gardener like that one, no one can replace

And I've been knocking but not one answers
And I've been knocking most all the day
Oh, and I've been calling 'Oh, hey hey Johnny
Can't you come out to play?'

And through their tears
Some say he farmed his best in younger years
But he'd have said that roots grow stronger if he could hear
Who lived there
He must have been a gardener that cared a lot
Who weeded out the tears and grew a good crop
Now we pray for rain, and with every drop that falls
We hear your name

And I've been knocking but no one answers
And I've been knocking most all the day
Oh, and I've been calling 'Oh, hey hey Johnny
Can't you come out to play?'

Johnny can't you come out to play?
Johnny in your empty garden?

empty sky

I'm not a rat to be spat upon
Locked up in this room
Those bars that look towards the sun
At night look towards the moon

Everyday the swallows play
In the clouds of love
Make me wish that I had wings
Take me high above

And I looked high
Saw the empty sky
If I could only
Could only fly

I'd drift with them
In endless space
But no man flies
From this place

At night I lay upon my bench
And stare towards the stars
The cold night air comes creeping in
And home seems oh so far

If I could only swing
Upon those twinkling dots above
I'd look down from the heavens
Upon the ones I love

Hey, the lucky locket
Hangs around your precious neck
Some luck I ever got with you
And I wouldn't like to bet

That sooner or later you'll own
Just one half of this land
By shining your eyes on the wealth
Of every man

Just send up my love
Ain't seen nothing but tears
Now I've got myself
In this room for years

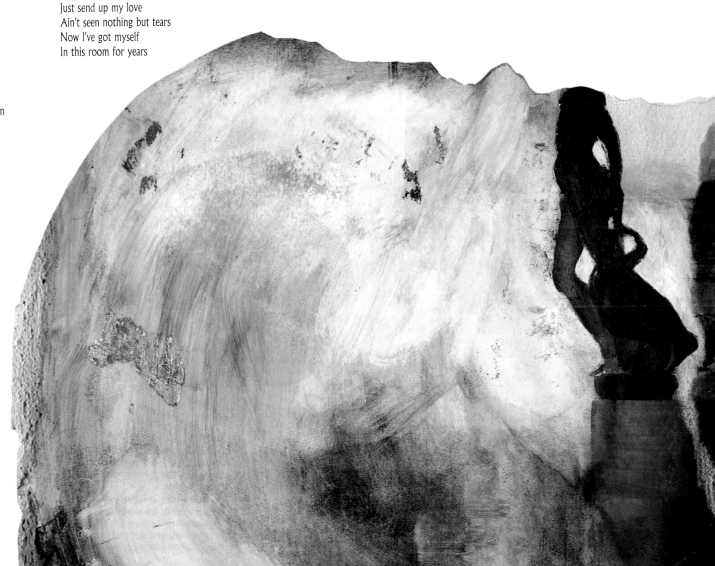

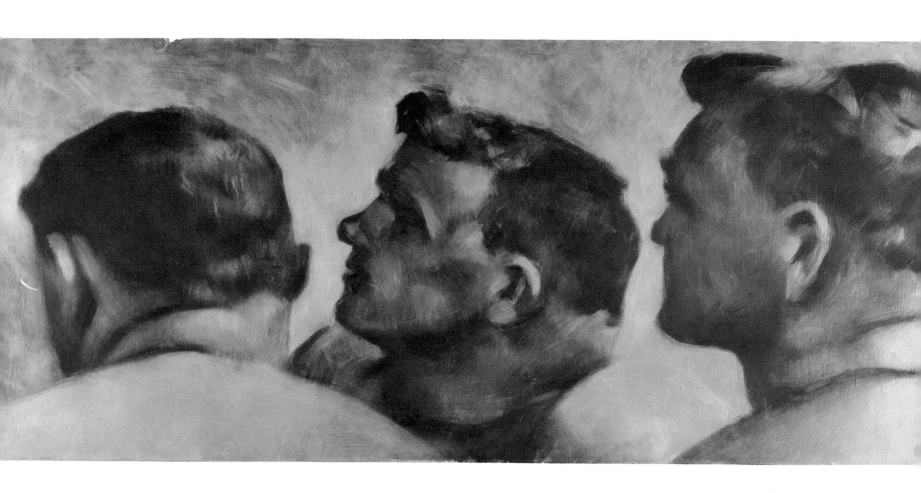

fascist faces

I read about how you're slow with the truth
Like any old Aesop's Fable
But when you're turtlesque, I'm a hare's breath
Into payment under the table
But some journalist got his mug shot kit
And his briefcase on his lap
But I'm tired of being linked with the K.G.B.
And all that political crap

'Cause I've seen your fascist faces
On the cover of the national papers
Staring out in black and white
From the tall grey walls on the other side
When I see your fascist faces
Then I know I've had enough
Trying to trace it or erase it
Is it foolproof or a bluff

If the boy'd been blessed he'd have been arrested
On a charge of wearin' red shoes
But if yer pants are blue you got nothing to lose
It'll make you a patriot through and through

fat boys
and ugly girls

Fat boys cry
When ugly girls sing
About the way the world would be
If they were thin.

And ugly girls turn their heads
When fat boys laugh
About the handsome kid next door
Who broke their heart.
Who broke their heart.
Broke their heart.

And fat boys lie
When ugly girls ask
About the size an apple pie looks
Through a magnifying glass
And ugly girls dream
At night when fat boys sleep
About the way the mirrors lie
When beauty's only skin deep
Beauty's only skin deep
Skin deep.

But it's the fat boy's world for an ugly girl
And ugly girls love that fat boy joy
Who needs the worries of a perfect world
Heart the early birds make that spring time come
When a fat boy falls in love with an ugly girl
When a fat boy falls in love with an ugly girl.

Fat boys dance
When ugly girls shout
That a waltz is not the dance for the boy who's stout
And ugly girls dream
At night when fat boys sleep
About the way the mirrors lie
When beauty's only skin deep
Beauty's only skin deep
Skin deep.

Fat boys
And ugly girls . . .

feed me

Don't close the shades
I'm scared of the darkness
I'm cold as a razor blade,
I'm inches from madness.

Don't let me sleep here,
They're all trying to kill me
I've seen the walls moving
They've all heard me screaming,
Screaming,

Feed me,
Feed my needs and then just leave me.
Let me go back where you found me
'Cause I miss my basement
The sweet smell of new paint
The warmth and comforts of home
So feed me
Give me my treatment and free me
My arms are so hungry so feed me.

The room's so distorted
And filled with mad shadows
I feel like a carcass
I'm white like a marrow bone.

It all seems so long ago
I remember them laughing,
I heard the ambulance scream
I saw the red light flashing, flashing.

first episode
at hienton

I was one as you were one
And we were two so much in love forever
I loved the white socks that you wore
But you don't wear white socks no more
Now you're a woman.

I joked about your turned-up nose
And criticized your school girl clothes
But would I then have paced these roads to love you.

For seasons come and seasons go
Bring forth the rain the sun and snow
Make Valerie a woman
And Valerie is lonely.

No more to roam on the snow hills of Hienton
Undecided with the guardians of the older generation
A doormat was a sign of welcome
In the winter months to come
And in the summer laughing
Through the castle ruins we'd run.

For the quadrangle sang to the sun,
And the grace of our feeling
And the candle burned low as we talked of the future
Underneath the ceiling.

There were tears in the sky
And the clouds in your eyes were just cover
For your thighs were the cushions
Of my love and yours for each other.

For seasons come and seasons go
Bring forth the rain the sun and snow
Make Valerie a woman
And Valerie is lonely.

The songs still are sung
It was fun to be young
But please don't be sad where'er you are
I am who I am
You are who you are
Now Valerie's a woman.

friends

I hope the day will be a lighter highway,
For friends are found on every road;
Can you ever think of any better way
For the lost and weary travellers to go?

Making friends for the world to see,
Let the people know you've got what you need;
With a friend at hand you will see the light,
If your friends are there, then everything's all right.

It seems to me a crime that we should age,
These fragile times should never slip us by;
A time you never can or shall erase
As friends together watch their childhood fly.

go it alone

It's so hard to say goodbye
When there's nothing left to give
When this house is just a hill of bones
Where you and I once lived
If we put it back together
By the skin of our teeth
You'd still pull it all apart
Bit by bit, piece by piece

And I'll go it alone
Call this house my home
Build it up again with someone new
Build it brick by brick
Till I find a girl that fits
This home's a whole lot better without you

There's no passion alive
When you count your phoney schemes
And the cars you drive to buy your friends
They don't ever come back clean
If the cards on the table
Always turn up spades
The cards that always cheat the hearts
The spades you play just dug my grave

And I'll go it alone
Call this house my home
Build it up again with someone new
Build it brick by brick
Till I find a girl that fits
This home's a whole lot better without you

goodbye

And now that it's all over.
The birds can nest again.
I'll only snow when the sun comes out,
I'll shine only when it starts to rain.

And if you want a drink,
Just squeeze my hand and wine will flow into the land
And feed my lambs.

For I am a mirror.
I can reflect the moon.
I will write songs for you.
I'll be your silver spoon.

I'm sorry I took your time.
I am the poem that doesn't rhyme.
Just turn back a page,
I'll waste away.

goodbye marlon brando

Say goodbye to loneliness
Say goodbye to Marlon Brando
Say goodbye to latitudes
And the confusion that surrounds you
Say goodbye to misery
Say goodbye to the morning news
Say goodbye to prime time
And the fools that choose to view
Say goodbye to Wendy
Say goodbye to Rhonda
Say goodbye to the Beach Boys
From the palisades to Kona.

Say goodbye to Glasnost
Say goodbye to Malathion
Say goodbye to the clones in congress
And the belt around Orion.
Say goodbye to the tabloids
Say goodbye to diet soda
Say goodbye to new age music
From the Capa to the Coda
Say goodbye to gridlock
Say goodbye to Dolly's chest
Say goodbye to the ozone layer
If there's any of it left.

Don't it make you wanna crawl back to the womb
Find a sanitarium and rent yourself a room
This overload is edging me further out to sea
I need to put some distance between overkill and me, me.

Say goodbye to Jackie Collins
Say goodbye to illiterate fools
Goodbye to evangelists
And geeks with power tools
Goodbye to statuettes
Say goodbye to lists
Say goodbye to articles
On who the senator kissed
Say goodbye to hairstyles
Goodbye to 'Heaven's Gate'
Goodbye to 'Rocky Five'
'Six' and 'seven' and 'eight'.

goodbye yellow brick road

When are you gonna come down?
When are you going to land?
I should have stayed on the farm,
I should have listened to my old man.

You know you can't hold me forever,
I didn't sign up with you.
I'm not a present for your friends to open,
This boy's too young to be singing the blues.

So goodbye yellow brick road,
Where the dogs of society howl.
You can't plant me in your penthouse,
I'm going back to my plough.

Back to the howling old owl in the woods,
Hunting the horny back toad,
Oh I've finally decided, my future lies
Beyond the yellow brick road.

What do you think you'll do then?
I bet that'll shoot down your plane.
It'll take you a couple of vodka and tonics
To set you on your feet again.

Maybe you'll get a replacement,
There's plenty like me to be found.
Mongrels, who ain't got a penny
Sniffing for tit-bits like you on the ground.

(gotta get a) meal ticket

I can hound you if I need to
Sip your brandy from a crystal shoe
In the corner, in the corner.
While others climb reaching dizzy heights,
The world's in front of me in black and white,
I'm on the bottom line, I'm on the bottom line.

I'd have a cardiac if I had such luck.
Lucky losers, lucky losers landing on skid row,
Landing on skid row.
While the Diamond Jims
And the Kings road pimps
Breathe heavy in their brand new clothes.
I'm on the bottom line, I'm on the bottom line.

And I gotta get a meal ticket
To survive you need a meal ticket,
To stay alive you need a meal ticket.
Feel no pain, no pain
No regret, no regret.
When the lines been signed
You're someone else.
Do yourself a favour and the meal ticket does the rest.

Shake a hand if you have to
Trust in us and we will love you
Anyway, anyway.
Don't leave us stranded in the jungle
With fifty per cent that's hard to handle,
Ain't that so, ain't that so.

grey seal

Why's it never light on my lawn
Why does it rain and never say good-day to the newborn?
On the big screen they showed us a sun,
But not as bright in life as the real one
It's never quite the same as the real one

And tell me grey seal
How does it feel
To be so wise
To see through eyes
That only see what's real
Tell me grey seal

I never learned why meteors were formed
I only farmed in schools that were so worn and torn
If anyone can cry then so can I
I read books and draw life from the eye.
All my life is drawings from the eye.

Your mission bells were wrought by ancient men
The roots were formed by twisted roots,
Your roots were twisted then
I was re-born before all life could die
The phoenix bird will leave this world to fly
If the phoenix bird can fly then so can I.

grimsby

As I lay dreaming in my bed
Across the great divide
I thought I heard the trawler boats
Returning on the tide
And in this vision of my home
The shingle beach did ring
I saw the lights along the pier
That made my senses sing.

Oh, Oh, Grimsby, a thousand delights
Couldn't match the sweet sights
Of my Grimsby
Oh, England you're fair
But there's none to compare
With my Grimsby
Through nights of mad youth
I have loved every sluice in your harbour
And in your wild sands
From boyhood to man
Strangers have found themselves fathers.

Take me back you rustic town
I miss your magic charm
Just to smell your candy floss
Or drink in the Skinners Arms
No Cordon Bleu can match the beauty
Of your pies and peas
I want to ride your fairground
Take air along the quay.

grow some funk of your own   gulliver / hay chewed / reprise

Well I looked at my watch and it said a quarter to five
The headlines screamed that I was still alive
I couldn't understand it
I thought I died last night.

I dreamed I'd been in a border town
In a little cantina that the boys had found,
I was desperate to dance
Just to dig the local sounds.

When along came a señorita
She looked so good that I had to meet her
I was ready to approach her
With my English charm,
When her brass-knuckled boyfriend
Grabbed my by the arm.

And he said grow some funk of your own, amigo
Grow some funk of your own
We no like to with the gringo fight,
But there might be a death in Mexico tonight
If you can't grow some funk of your own, amigo,
Grow some funk of your own
Take my advice, take the next flight,
And grow some funk, grow your funk at home.

Well I looked for support from the rest of my friends
For their vanishing trick they get ten out of ten
I knelt to pray
Just to see if he would comprehend.

Gulliver's gone
To the final command of his master
His watery eyes had washed
All the hills with his laughter
And the seasons can change
All the light from the grey to the dim
But the light in his eyes
Will see no more so bright,
As the sheep
That he locked in the pen

There's four feet of ground
In front of the barn
That's sun-baked, and rain-soaked
And part of the farm
But now it lies empty
So cold and so bare
Gulliver's gone
But his memory lies there

By passing the doors of his life
Was a stage I remember
And in later years
He would cease to bare teeth to a stranger
For sentiment touched him
As cyclamen holds him

And later, men came from the town
Who said, clear the child
This won't take a while
And Gulliver's gone with the dawn

gypsy heart

You win again you, gypsy heart
I count the days that we're apart
I sleep alone when you're away
No sense in saying 'I wish you'd stay'
It's all the same, you never change
You come and go just like the rain
I pray each day that you are gone
This time it won't be so long

Your gypsy heart will never find
Any arms as warm as mine
And gypsy when we meet again
I'll play my part
And wrap you up inside my arms oh you gypsy heart
Your gypsy heart can always call
When you back's against the wall
And darlin' then I'll just pretend
Right from the start
You never left me on my own oh you gypsy heart

I pray each day that you are gone
This time oh it won't be so long

Your gypsy heart will never find
Any arms as warm as mine
And gypsy when we meet again
I'll play my part
And wrap you up inside my arms oh you gypsy heart
Your gypsy heart can always call
When you back's against the wall
And darlin' then I'll just pretend
Right from the start
You never left me on my own oh you gypsy heart

hard luck story

Sometimes I think I'm going crazy
Staring at the same four walls
Waiting for the working day to end.
Then I get home so wasted, worn out
Curse at you and tell you
How I've done the work of ten to fifteen men
How I've struggled for my money
Sweated blood to get us by
Well I'm tired of it honey
Think I'm gonna have to leave here for a while.

Ooee ooee ooh all you hear are hard luck stories
Ooee ooee ooh and the ways I look at life.
Ooee ooee ooh and the way I think the world treats me
Ooee ooee ooh and the way that I treat my wife.

I never seem to look at you
And see that somewhere underneath
A pair of tired eyes are crying out.
Well you know I work hard all day long
Let me kiss you once with meaning
Just to kill this nagging doubt.
Well you don't deny I do you proud
And you expect me to be tired
You say there's no future in our lives
While I persist I'm putting out the fire.

Ooee ooee ooh all you hear are hard luck stories
Ooee ooee ooh just a few well chosen words
Ooee ooee ooh cause you're the woman of a working man
Ooee ooee ooh you've got the heart of a working girl.

harmony

Hello, baby hello,
Haven't seen your face for a while.
Have you quit doing time for me,
Or are you still the same spoilt child?

Hello, I said hello,
Is this the only place you thought to go?
Am I the only man you ever had,
Or am I just the last surviving friend that you know?

Harmony and me
We're pretty good company,
Looking for an island
In our boat upon the sea.
Harmony, gee I really love you
And I want to love you forever
And dream of the never, never, never leaving harmony.
Hello, baby hello,
Open up your heart and let your feelings flow.
You're not unlucky knowing me,
Keeping the speed real slow.
In any case I set my own pace
By stealing the show, say hello, hello.

have mercy on the criminal

Have you heard, the dogs at night,
Somewhere on the hill,
Chasing some poor criminal,
And I guess they're out to kill.
Oh, there must be shackles, on his feet,
And mother, in his eyes, stumbling through the devil-dark,
With the hound pack in full cry.

Have mercy on the criminal,
Who is running from the law,
Are you blind to the
Winds of change?
Don't you hear him any more?

Praying Lord you gotta help me,
I am never gonna sin again,
Just take, these chains,
From around my legs,
Sweet Jesus I'll be your friend.

Now have you ever seen,
The white teeth gleam,
While you lie on a
Cold damp ground,
You're taking in the face of a rifle butt,
While the wardens hold you down,
And you've never seen a friend in years.
Oh, it turns your heart to stone,
You jump the walls.
And the dogs run free,
And the grave's gonna be your home.

healing hands

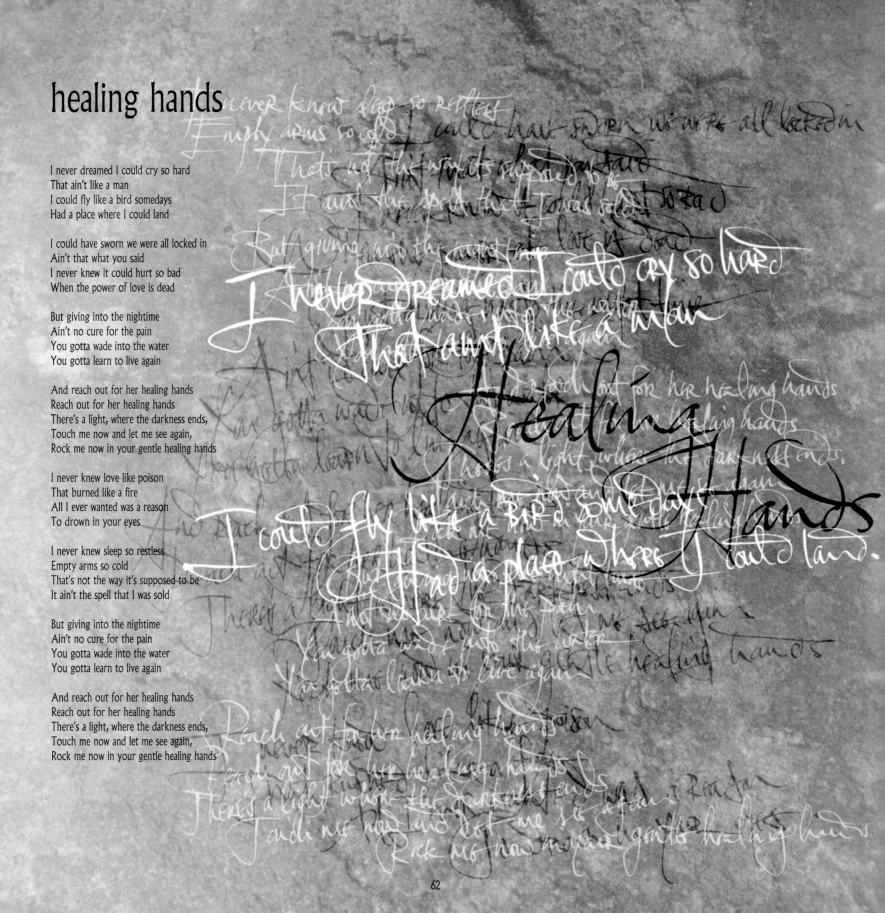

I never dreamed I could cry so hard
That ain't like a man
I could fly like a bird somedays
Had a place where I could land

I could have sworn we were all locked in
Ain't that what you said
I never knew it could hurt so bad
When the power of love is dead

But giving into the nightime
Ain't no cure for the pain
You gotta wade into the water
You gotta learn to live again

And reach out for her healing hands
Reach out for her healing hands
There's a light, where the darkness ends,
Touch me now and let me see again,
Rock me now in your gentle healing hands

I never knew love like poison
That burned like a fire
All I ever wanted was a reason
To drown in your eyes

I never knew sleep so restless
Empty arms so cold
That's not the way it's supposed to be
It ain't the spell that I was sold

But giving into the nightime
Ain't no cure for the pain
You gotta wade into the water
You gotta learn to live again

And reach out for her healing hands
Reach out for her healing hands
There's a light, where the darkness ends,
Touch me now and let me see again,
Rock me now in your gentle healing hands

Well I'm running away
From this house on the hill
There's a devil inside
Sitting on the window sill
And it's a wild Friday night
And I'm all on my own
I knocked on every door in town
There ain't one little girl that's home
And everybody's got a date
And the ones that ain't are tired
What the hell do you do on a weekend honey
When you heart's on fire

And you can go from Tokyo to Rome
Looking for a girl
But it looks to me like the weekend means
Heartache all over the world
Girls girls girls
Have pity on me
Oh it looks to me like the weekend means
Heartache, heartache all over the world

He's got lipstick on his collar
She's got fishnets on her legs
I'm at home and I've got nothin'
Just a cold and aching head
There must be something dirty
Just blame it on the magazines
Don't read that trash it'll drive you crazy
'Cause the cops invade your dreams
And everybody's got a date
And the ones that ain't are tired
What the hell do you do on a weekend honey
When your heart's on fire

And you can go from Tokyo to Rome
Looking for a girl
But it seems to me like the weekend means
Heartache all over the world
Girls girls girls
Have pity on me
Oh it seems to me like the weekend means
Heartache, heartache all over the world

heavy traffic

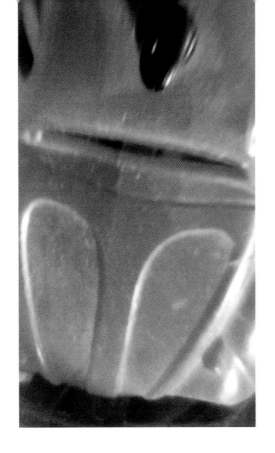

Shakey wake up thirsty from a night in the bar
And snake hips Joe is Mr. Cool
Out on the boulevard
The pimp from the Jack of Diamond
Got another Jane Doe
She just got off the last bus from Montecedo.

Sailor boys find trouble in the alien state
It's one on one from Los Palmas to the Golden Gate
Fly boys on the corner waiting for a ride
For twenty bucks he'll pull in the plug on the man inside.

'Cause we're rolling in heavy traffic
Judy's in the jump seat and Jody's in the bucket
Billy likes to drive, Jackie's just high
Cindy thinks we're all gonna commit suicide.
'Cause we're rolling in heavy traffic.

Mack he's got his Marlboros tucked up in his sleeve
He's shacked up in the basement making P.C.P.
He used to shake the French fries
Down on 12th and Maine
And now he stays up nights on apple juice and cocaine.

'Cause we're rolling in heavy traffic
Judy's in the jump seat and Jody's in the bucket
Billy likes to drive, Jackie's just high
And Cindy thinks we're all gonna commit suicide.
'Cause we're rolling in heavy traffic.

heels of the wind

Just like a broken marriage, when two people just don't care
Like when the cupboard is empty or there's no food in the Frigidaire
I'm a page from the end of the story
No closer to my hope and glory
Just a kick away from the heels of the wind

How come it gets so disturbing, when two ships pass in the storm
Who knows how high the crow flies, who know where this refugee was born
I'm a page from the end of the story
No closer to my hope and glory
Just a kick away from the heels of the wind

And just for the sake of all these reasons
Rains wash out the fires within
Fire that helps to keep you moving
Just a kick away from the heels of the wind

You don't deserve that treatment, I can't pretend I was that nice
I'm no E ticket ride to Disneyland, I'm no cushy first-class flight
I'm a day behind your restless wings
You, you, rather have the wealth of kings
Me, I'd rather be on the heels of the wind

hercules

Ooh, I got a busted wing
And a hornet sting
Like an out of tune guitar.
Oh, she got Hercules on her side
And Diana in her eyes.

Some men like the Chinese life,
Some men kneel and pray.
Well, I like women
And I like wine
And I've always liked it that way,
Always liked it that way.

But I can't dig it,
The way she tease
That old tough man routine up her sleeve,
Livin' and a'lovin', kissin' and a'huggin',
Livin' and a'lovin' with a cat named Hercules.

Oh, and it hurts like hell,
To see my gal
Messin' with a muscle boy,
No superman gonna ruin my plans
Playin' with my toys.

Rich man sweatin' in a sauna bath,
Poor boy scrubbin' in a tub,
Me, I stay gritty up to my ears,
Washing in a bucket of mud,
Washing in a bucket of mud.

high-flying bird

You wore a little cross of gold around your neck,
I saw it as you flew between my reason,
Like a raven in the night time when you left.
I wear a chain upon my wrist that bears no name,
You touched it and you wore it,
And you kept it in your pillow, all the same.

My high-flying bird has flown from out my arms,
I thought myself her keeper,
She thought I meant her harm,
She thought I was the archer,
A weather man of words,
But I could never shoot down,
My high-flying bird.

The white walls of your dressing room are stained in scarlet red.
You bled upon the cold stone like a young man,
In the foreign field of death.
Wouldn't it be wonderful is all I heard you say,
You never closed your eyes at night and learnt to love daylight,
Instead, you moved away.

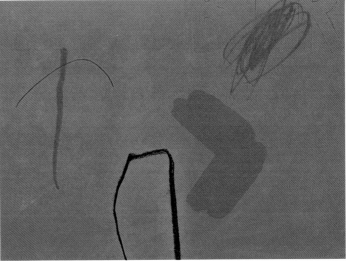

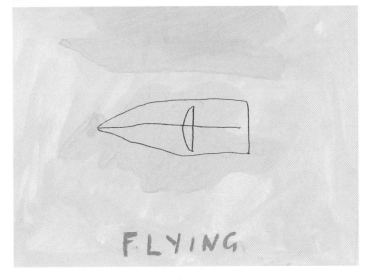

holiday inn

Boston at last
And the plane's touching down.
Our hostess is handing
The hot towels around.
From a terminal gate
To a black limousine.
It's a ten minute ride
To the Holiday Inn.

Boredom's a pastime
That one soon acquired,
Where you get to the stage
Where you're not even tired.
Kicking your heels
Till the time comes around
To pick up your bags
And head out of town.

Slow down Joe,
I'm a rock 'n roll man.
I've twiddled my thumbs
In a dozen odd bands,
And you ain't seen nothing
Until you've been in
A motel baby
Like the Holiday Inn.

ho ho ho, who 'd be a turkey at christmas

Sitting here on Christmas Eve
With a brandy in my hand
I've had a few too many
And it's getting hard to stand
Lots of crackling noises
From my fireplace
I must be going crazy
Or that brandy's won the race

And I keep hearing ho ho ho guess who's here
The fat and jolly friend appears
Ho ho ho surprise surprise
The bearded weirdo's just arrived

On my roof there's thumping sounds
And bells inside my head
My vision's blurred with colour
And all I see is red
Massive wellies coming down my flue
And the smell of burning rubber
Starts to fill the room

I keep hearing ho ho ho guess who's here
The fat and jolly friend appears
Ho ho ho surprise surprise
The bearded weirdo's just arrived

And we keep hearing ho ho ho guess who's here
The fat and jolly friend appears
Ho ho ho surprise surprise
The bearded weirdo's just arrived

honey roll

Do you want to drive to ride mount on your pony
Loosen up my tie to help me breathe
Insisting that I pay my alimony
Each and every day is the same old scene

Come on do the roll do the roll with me
Come on do the roll do the roll with me
I said honey, yeh honey, hey honey I said honey
Come on do the honey roll with me

Well I want to say that I'm funky
Singing this song is taking up your time
I did the donkey now I'm your funky monkey
Sing it child yeh sing it on your mind

Come on do the roll do the roll with me
Come on do the roll do the roll with me
I said honey, hey honey, hey honey I said honey
Come on do the honey roll with me

honky cat

When I look back,
Boy, I must have been green,
Boppin' in the country,
Fishin' in a stream.

Lookin' for an answer,
Tryin' to find a sign,
Until I saw your city lights,
Honey, I was blind.

They said, get back, Honky Cat,
Better get back to the woods,
Well, I quit those days and my redneck ways,
And oh, oh, oh, oh, the change is gonna do me good.

You better get back, Honky Cat,
Livin' in the city ain't where it's at.
It's like tryin' to find gold in a silver mine,
It's like tryin' to drink whisky from a bottle of wine.

Well I read some books, and I read some magazines
About those high class ladies
Down in New Orleans,
And all the folks back home said I was a fool,
They said, believe in the Lord,
Is the golden rule.

They said stay at home, boy, you gotta tend the farm,
Livin' in the city, boy,
Is gonna break your heart.
But how can you stay, when your heart says no,
How can you stop,
When your feet say go.

hoop of fire

You say that all you want are the simple things —
Long walks on lonely beaches, guitars with nylon strings
But underneath you'd rather leap through a hoop of fire
You shy away from lips that want, that want to kiss you
Tongue-tied on formal evenings, wealth don't impress you
But if you ask me you like the heat in a hoop of fire

And it's hard to read just how you feel
Or what your dreams desire
Your pulse that races when I'm close
Reads like a hoop of fire
Your pulse that races when I'm close
Reads like a hoop of fire

No late nights making love in secret places
You feel pressure all around you, mistrust in strangers' faces
But don't pretend you wouldn't spend some time in a hoop of fire

But don't pretend you wouldn't spend some time in a hoop of fire

house

This is my house
This is where I live
That is the winter
Those are the trees
I can hear them breathe
This is my bed
This is where I sleep
That was the dark
Those are my dreams
They belong to me

This is my floor
This is where I lie
This is a square room
That was a bright light
These are not my eyes
What is my soul?
Where is my tired heart?
That is the question
Where is the answer?
Inside my house

And I sit by the window
And I wish I was rain
I want to fall from the sky
I want to get wet all over again

'Cause this is my house
It belongs to me
Inside my head
It's all that's left
This is my house
This is my bed
This is where I sleep
That was the dark
Those are my dreams
They belong to me

This is my house
This is my house
This is my house
Yeah this is my house

house of cards

I hear tales that a playboy has kidnapped your heart
With his plane and his plans for games after dark
Just his pen in his pocket and the price of a room
Where the second-hand sheets smell of stale perfume

If there's sharks in the water don't swim where its deep
For the success can be bitter and sweet
It could be you're right that I act like a child
Oh but you'll be the loser when the joke has run wild

You're just playing the game but the stakes are too high
What will you do when the chips start to fly
When the deck is stacked against you and the living gets hard
Well there's much talk of madness in this house of cards

Come on and call me 'cause I know there's time
In a handful of diamonds or a heart so divine
And your house of cards starts weighing me down
The nights become restless when the cards start to come down

You're just playing the game but the stakes are too high
What will you do when the chips start to fly
When the deck is stacked against you and the living gets hard
Well there's much talk of madness in this house of cards

hymn 2000

She chose the soft centre
And took it to bed with her mother
And the ideal confusion
Was just an illusion
To gain further news of her brother

And the comfort of mother
Was just an appeal for protection
For the cat from next door
Was found later at four
In surgical dissection

And I don't want to be
The son of any freak
Who for a chocolate centre
Can take you off the street

For soon they'll plough the desert
And God knows where I'll be
Collecting submarine numbers
On the main street of the sea

The vicar is thicker
And I just can't see through to him
For his cardinal sings
A collection of hymns
And a collection of coins
Is made after

And who wrote the Bible
Was it Judas or Pilate
Well one cleans his hands
While the other one hangs
But still I continue to stand

I am your robot

I've been beaming aboard her for a light year, from a strange craft
She's got a subtle touch on the silver key to a clockwork heart
I am your robot, I am your robot
I am your robot man

You went and flipped the switch and turned me positive when I was negative
I've been stumbling around like a metal man, on the graveyard shift
I am your robot, I am your robot
I am your robot man

I am your robot and I'm programmed to love you
My serial number is 44357
I am your robot, I am your robot
I am your robot man

I cry at night

This house that I live in has no reason
This house that I live in has no purpose
It has a bed and a few old chairs
Three flights up two flights of stairs
But it has no reason

Someone shot through the tyre swing
And the dog barks and
There's a change in the weather and spring
And the ivy that hung outside the drains
To a dying season

Night light night when the lights go out
And the green eyes fuse and the full moon shines
From road maps and red lines to lipstick lies
And when the lights go out it's tough to survive

This man holds a hand which shows a tremble
This man that I live in bears his faults
He has a heart and a well worn soul
Ten years a slave to rock 'n' roll but he has to tremble

For the yellow grass on the sun burnt lawn
Sleeps in the seed from the sunset till dawn
And just like your love that's come and gone
It goes on breathing

idol

Oh, he was a light star
Tripping on a high wire
Bulldog stubborn, born uneven,
A classless creature, a man for all seasons
But don't bet them
That they can't take him
To the very bottom.
'Cause they made him and they'll waste him
And I don't believe that I want to watch them.

'Cause the fifties shifted out of gear
He was an idol then, now he's an idol here
But his face has changed, he's not the same no-more
And I have to say that I like the way his music sounded
before.

He was tight-assed
Walking on broken glass
Highly prized in the wallet size
The number one crush in a schoolgirl's eyes.
But don't pretend that it won't end
In the depth of your despair
You went from lamé suits right down to tennis shoes,
To peanuts from the lion's share.

I don't wanna go on with you like that

I've always said that one's enough to love
Now I hear you braggin' one is not enough
Oh! Something tells me you're not satisfied
You got plans to make me one of four or five.

I guess this kind of thing's just in your blood
But you won't catch me carving up my love
I ain't no puzzle piece that needs to fit
If it takes more than me let's call it quits.

'Cause I don't wanna go on with you like that
Don't wanna be a feather in your cap
I just wanna tell you honey I ain't mad
But I don't wanna go on with you like that.

Woh oh oh, woh oh, woh oh, oh yeah.

It gets so hard sometimes to understand
This vicious circle's getting out of hand
Don't need an extra eye to see
That the fire spreads faster in a breeze.

And I don't wanna go on with you like that
Don't wanna be a feather in your cap
I just wanna tell you honey I ain't mad
But I don't wanna go on with you like that
I don't wanna go on with you like that.
One more set of boots on your welcome mat
You'll just have to quit 'em if you want me back
'Cause I don't wanna go on with you like that.

Woh oh oh, woh oh, woh oh, oh yeah.

Oh! If you wanna spread it around sister that's just fine
But I don't want no second hand feeding me lines
If you wanna hold someone in the middle of the night
Call out the guards, turn out the light.

And I don't wanna go on with you like that
Don't wanna be a feather in your cap
I just wanna tell you honey I ain't mad
But I don't wanna go on with you like that
No I don't wanna go on with you like that
One more set of boots on your welcome mat
You'll just have to quit 'em if you want me back
No I don't wanna go on with you like that.

I fall apart

Without you I no longer swim upstream
Where are you when I try to fill the spaces in-between
The red letter days and all the pain
And while I remain shipwrecked everything has changed

And I fall apart
With this threat of indecision
Hanging in my heart
This house can get so lonely
When the day grows dark
And it seems to be the night time
When I fall apart

Can't you tell the shadows no longer comfort me
I don't feel the need to cling to anyone I see
This fool's suffered gladly each and every day
I don't wish to reconsider, I wish they'd stay away

I've not a care to count
The stares that pity me
I'll wash your hurt away
Just you wait and see
For every rose he gives her
I'll give her three
But in the meantime
I'll just wish that he was me

And I fall apart
With this threat of indecision
Hanging in my heart
This house can get so lonely
When the day grows dark
And it seems to be the night time
When I fall apart

I fall apart I fall apart
This house can get so lonely
Oh when the day grows dark
And it seems to be the night time
That I fall apart

I feel like a bullet
(in the gun of robert ford)

Like corn in a field I cut you down
I threw the last punch too hard,
After years of going steady,
Well I thought it was time
To throw in my hand for a new set of cards.

And I can't take you dancing out on the weekend
I figured we'd painted too much of this town,
And I tried not to look as I walked to my wagon
And I knew then I had lost what should have been found
I knew then I had lost what should have been found.

And I feel like a bullet in the gun of Robert Ford
I'm low as a paid assassin is
You know I'm cold as a hired sword.
I'm so ashamed we can't patch it up

You know I can't think straight no more
You make me feel like a bullet honey
In the gun of Robert Ford.

Like a child when his toy's been stepped on
That's how it all seemed to me,
I burst the bubble that both of us lived in
And I'm damned if I'll ever get rid of
This guitar that I feel.

And if looks could kill I'd be a dead man
Your friends and mine don't call anymore
Hell, I thought it was best but now I feel branded,
Breaking up's sometimes like breaking the law
Breaking up's sometimes like breaking the law.

if there's a god in heaven (what's he waiting for)

Torn from their families,
Mothers go hungry,
To feed their children,
But children go hungry,
There's so many big men
Out making millions
When poverty's profits
Just blame the children.

If there's a God in Heaven
What's He waiting for?
If He can't hear the children,
Then He must see the war,
But it seems to me
That He leads his lambs
To the slaughter house
Not the promised land.

Dying for causes
They don't understand.
We've been taking their futures
Right out of their hands.
They need the handouts
To hold back the tears,
There's so many crying
But so few that hear.

I guess that's why they call it the blues

Don't wish it away
Don't look at it like it's forever
Between you and me
I could honestly say
That things can only get better

And while I'm away
Dust out the demons inside
And it won't be long,
Before you and me run
To the place in our hearts
Where we hide

And I guess that's why
They call it the blues
Time on my hands
Could be time spent with you
Laughing like children,
Living like lovers
Rolling like thunder under the covers
And I guess that's why
They call it the blues

Just stare into space
Picture my face in your hands
Live for each second
Without hesitation
And never forget I'm your man

Wait on me girl
Cry in the night if it helps
But more than ever I simply love you
More than I love life itself

And I guess that's why
They call it the blues
Time on my hands
Could be time spent with you
Laughing like children,
Living like lovers
Rolling like thunder under the covers
And I guess that's why
They call it the blues

I'm going to be a teenage idol

Well there's slim times when my words won't rhyme,
And the hills I face are a long hard climb,
I just sit cross legged with my old guitar,
Ooh, it kind of makes me feel like a rock and roll star.

Well it makes me laugh Lord it makes me cry,
And I think for once let me just get high,
Let me get electric put a silk suit on,
Turn my old guitar into a tommy gun.

And root, toot, shoot, myself to fame,
Every kid alive gonna know my name,
An overnight phenomenon, like there's never been,
A motivated supersonic king of the scene.

I'll be a teenage idol, just give me a break,
I'm gonna be a teenage idol, no matter how long it takes,
You can't imagine what it means to me,
I'm gonna grab myself a place in history,
A teenage idol that's what I'm gonna be.

Well life is short and the world is rough,
And if you're gonna boogie boy you gotta be tough,
Nobody knows if I'm dead or alive,
I just drink myself to sleep each night.

And so I pray to the teenage god of rock,
If I make it big let me stay on top,
You gotta cut me loose from this one room dive,
Put me on the ladder keep this boy alive.

I'm still standing

You could never know what it's like
Your blood like winter freezes
Just like ice and there's cold
Lonely light that shines from you
You'll wind up like
The wreck you hide
Behind that mask you use

And did you think
This fool could never win
Well look at me,
I'm a comin' back again
I got a taste of love
In a simple way
And if you need to know,
While I'm still standing
You just fade away

Don't you know, I'm still standing
Better than I ever did
Lookin' like a true survivor
Feelin' like a little kid
I'm still standing
After all this time
Pickin' up the pieces of my life
Without you on my mind

I'm still standing, yea yea yea
I'm still standing, yea yea yea

Once I could never hope to win
You starting down the road,
Leaving me again
The threats you made
Were meant to cut me down
And if our love was just a circus
You'd be a clown by now

Born 1769.
Died 1821.
at St Helena.

indian sunset

As I awoke this evening with the smell of woodsmoke clinging.
Like a gentle cobweb hanging upon a painted tepee.
Oh I went to see my chieftain with my war lance and my woman.
For he told us that the yellow moon would very soon be leaving.

This I can't believe I said, I can't believe our Warlord's dead.
Oh, he would not leave the chosen ones to the buzzards and the soldiers' guns.

Oh, great father of the Iroquois ever since I was young,
I've read the writing of the smoke and breast-fed on the sound of drums.
I've learned to hurl the tomahawk and ride a painted pony wild.
To run the gauntlet of the Sioux, to make a chieftain's daughter mine.

And now you ask that I should watch the red man's race be slowly crushed!
What kind of words are these to hear from Yellow Dog, whom white man fears?

I take only what is mine Lord, my pony, my squaw, and my child.
I can't stay to see you die along with my tribe's pride.
I got to search for the yellow moon and the Fathers of our sons,
Where the red sun sinks in the hills of gold and the healing waters run.

Trampling down the prairie rose, leaving hoof tracks in the sand.
Those who wish to follow me, I welcome with my hands.
I heard from passing renegades Geronimo was dead,
He'd been laying down his weapons when they filled him full of lead.

Now there seems no reason why I should carry on,
In this land that once was my land, I can't find a home.
It's lonely and it's quiet and the horse soldiers are coming,
And I think it's time I strung my bow and ceased my senseless running.
For soon I'll find the yellow moon, along with my loved ones.
Where the buffaloes graze in clover fields without the sound of guns.

And the red sun sinks at last into the hills of gold
And peace to this young warrior comes with a bullet hole.

I need you to turn to

You're not a ship to carry my life
You are nailed to my love in many lonely nights.

I've strayed from the cottages and found myself here
For I need your love, your love protects my fears.

And I wonder sometimes and I know I'm unkind
But I need you to turn to when I act so blind
And I need you to turn to when I lose control
You're my guardian angel who keeps out the cold.

Did you paint your smile on? well I said I knew
That my reason for living was for loving you.

We're related in feeling but you're high above
You're pure and you're gentle with the grace of a dove.

I never knew her name

Well she swept through the church
Like a sweet Sunday prayer
While the choir sang 'Son Of Heaven'
And the groom just walked on air

I was killing time with Jesus
When the wedding bells began
And I saw the most beautiful woman
Getting married to a handsome man

And she walked like a mystery
And she passed like summer rain
And she said 'I do' like an angel
But I never knew her name

Oh the congregation gathered
But in darkness I remained
In love with the bride of a handsome man
But I never knew her name

In the shadow of the holy
Oh I heard my tell-tale heart
Whisper words that never reached her
As her vows were made at last

Oh! the preacher with his blessing
Pronounced them man and wife
And I saw the most beautiful woman
Make a promise to be kept for life

And she walked like a mystery
And she passed like summer rain
And she said 'I do' like an angel
But I never knew her name

Oh the congregation gathered
But in darkness I remained
In love with the bride of a handsome man
But I never knew her name

And she walked like a mystery
And she passed like a summer rain
And she said 'I do' like an angel
But I never knew her name

in neon

Lipstick and lashes, the traces of stardom
Lit up on a billboard so everyone sees them in neon
Behind a counter she stares out the window
Up at the billboard that's like a reminder in neon

She hates how she feels but she hangs like a mirror
Maybe a stranger could walk in and see her in neon
For two cents of danger she'd trust anybody
She'd smoke like a gun if it meant she might wind up
In neon the dreams in the light of a promise that dies
A shimmering city, a glimmer of hope and a lie
In neon the name's gone there's no reason why anymore
Trust them and wind up alone behind a locked door

In neon, in neon. . .

Pictures and patterns, the touches of glamour
Cut into fashion that flashes above 'em in neon
A hot cup of coffee held in her fingers
A perfect complexion that lingers above her in neon

She hates how she feels but she hangs like a mirror
Maybe a stranger could walk in and see her in neon
For a shot at the title, she'd slip into something
She'd smoulder like ashes if it meant she might wind up

In neon. . .

into the old man's shoes

I'm moving out of Tombstone
With the sun behind my back,
I'm tired of people talking
Of the things that I did lack.
Ever since a week ago,
The day he passed away,
I've been taking too much notice
Of the things they've had to say.

And all they say
Is – you ain't half the man he used to be,
He had strength and worked his life
To feed his family.
So if that's the way it has to be,
I'll say goodbye to you,
I'm not the guy, or so it seems,
To fill my old man's shoes.

Like I'm a wicked way of life,
The kind that must be tamed,
They'd like to see me locked in jail
And tied up in their chains.
Oh! It's hard, and I can't see
What they want me to do, Lord,
They seem to think
I should step into my old man's shoes.

island girl

I see your teeth flash
Jamaican honey so sweet
Down where Lexington cross 47th Street
She's a big girl, she's standing six foot three
Turning tricks for the dudes in the big city.

Island girl,
What you wantin' wid de white man's world
Island girl
Black boy want you in his island world.
He want to take you from de racket Boss,
He want to save you but de cause is lost.
Island girl, island girl, island girl
Tell me what you wantin' wid de white man's world.

She's black as coal
But she burn like a fire
And she wrap herself around you
Like a well worn tyre.
You feel her nail scratch your back just like a rake,
He one more gone, he one more john who make de mistake.

I swear I heard the night talking

In the nicotine glare of a cold naked light
I drag my body from the covers and down forty flights.
I run out the front door into the center of the street,
I scream out your name as the scene just swells around my feet.

I hear you after midnight from the inner city
As ev'ry little Cinderella turns to drop dead pretty.
We were built out of the darkness into this West Side Story
We came together in the shadows but the moon just steals our glory.

Well this is my battleground, baby.
This is my plaything.
The only thing I've ever known.

On the burden of insanity, we can't find the cause.
On the flat bed truck well the home girl she paints her claws.
There's a coward who gets his courage undercover of the dark.
And it's a strange breed of devil freeze at night to go walkin' in the park.

I think I'm going to kill myself

I'm getting bored
Being part of mankind,
There's not a lot to do no more,
This race is a waste of time.

People rushing everywhere,
Swarming round like flies,
Think I'll buy a forty-four,
Give 'em all a surprise.

Think I'm gonna kill myself,
Cause a little suicide,
Stick around for a couple of days,
What a scandal if I died.

Yea, I'm gonna kill myself,
Get a little headline news.
I'd like to see what the papers say
On the state of teenage blues.

A rift in my family,
I can't use the car,
I gotta be in by ten o'clock,
Who do they think they are?

I'd make an exception
If you want to save my life,
Brigitte Bardot gotta come
And see me every night.

it's me that you need

Hey there – look in the mirror,
Are you afraid you might see me looking at you?
Waiting, waiting at windows,
Oh, it's me that you need.
Yes, it's me, and I'm waiting for you.

But I'll remain silent,
Oh, I won't say a word,
I'll leave you to realize
I'm the light in your world.

And it's me, yes, it's me,
Yes, it's me, yes, it's me, that you're needing,
It's me, yes, it's me,
Yes, it's me, yes, it's me that you need.
Yes, it's me, yes, it's me,
Yes, it's me if you want to be living,
I'm the one who's forgiving,
Admit that it's me that you need.

Watching, watching the swallows fly,
It all means the same.
Just like them, you can fly home again
But don't, don't forget yesterday,
Pride is an ugly word, girl,
And you still know my name.

I've been loving you

I didn't mean to hurt you
You know it's just my way
Those things that I said yesterday
Were things I shouldn't say
Although you're blue
Just one thing I want you to do
Just forget all those things
That I said about you

'Cause I've been loving you baby
Loving you baby for a long time
And if you go away
I just won't know what to do
Yes I've been loving you baby
Loving you for a long time
And you know in your heart
That I've always worshipped you
I couldn't bear to see you go
Oh no no no no no

So don't feel sad
It's not the thing to do
Because I worry
If I know you're feeling blue
Please put your tears away
So nobody can see
'Cause the last thing I want
Is for you to cry over me

'Cause I've been loving you baby
Loving you baby for a long time
And if you go away
I just won't know what to do
Yes I've been loving you baby
Loving you for a long time
And you know in your heart
That I've always worshipped you
I couldn't bear to see you go
Oh no no no no no

I've seen that movie too

I can see by your eyes you must be lying
When you think I don't have a clue.
Baby you're crazy
If you think that you can fool me,
Because I've seen that movie too.

The one where the players are acting surprised
Saying love's just a four letter word.
Between forcing smiles, with the knives in their eyes,
Well their actions become so absurd.

So keep your auditions for somebody
Who hasn't got so much to lose.
'Cause you can tell by the lines I'm reciting,
That I've seen that movie too.

It's a habit I have, I don't get pushed around
Stop twinkling your star like you do.
I'm not the blue-print
For all of your B films,
Because I've seen that movie too.

I've seen the saucers

Tune in, wouldn't it be something
Rumours spreading into panic
I've seen movements in the clearing
Someone sent you something satanic.

I have to leave you, radar's calling
Outside somebody landed
Crazy wavelengths leave you helpless
Oh, don't forget me, I'm so stranded.

I wouldn't fool you but I've seen the saucers
So many times I'm almost in tune
Watching them flying in formation
Thinking how I could be so immune.

I've seen them, I've been there with them
I can tell you all you want to know
Something touched me, and I was only sleeping
Wouldn't you, wouldn't you, like to go.

Stars climbing into their planets
Systems won, controlled from birth
Empty living on this highway
Can you see me mother earth.

It's so endless whirling onwards
Wonder what's cookin' at home tonight
Maybe if I promise not to say a word
They can get me back before the morning light.

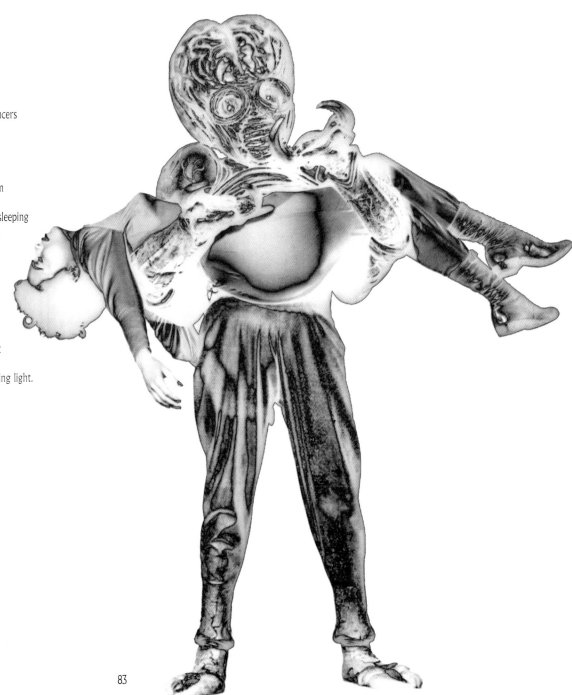

jack-rabbit

Go, jack-rabbit, running through the wood,
You had a good night and you feel real loose,
Heard they got you going round the goosecreek shed,
Trying to fill your belly full of buckshot lead.

Go, jack-rabbit, get the cabbage patch,
Farmer left the back porch door on the latch,
Heard you coming and he got his gun,
Better go, jack-rabbit, better start to run.

Go, jack-rabbit, running through the woods,
You had a good night and you feel real loose,
Gunfire breaking up the peaceful night
Jack-rabbit lying in the cold daylight.

jamaica jerk-off

When she gets up in the morning
It's enough to wake the dead,
Oh she turning on the radio
And dancing on my head.

It's no good living in the sun
Playing guitar all day,
Boogalooin' with my friends
In that erotic way.

Come on Jamaica
In Jamaica all day,
Dancing with your darling
Do Jamaica jerk-off that way.

Come on Jamaica
Everybody say,
We're all happy in Jamaica
Do Jamaica jerk-off that way.

Let the ladies and the gentlemen
Be as rude as they like —
On the beaches, oh in the jungle,
Where the people feel all right.

So do it in Jamaica
Got plenty for you and me,
Honky tonkin' with my baby
In the deep blue sea.

japanese hands

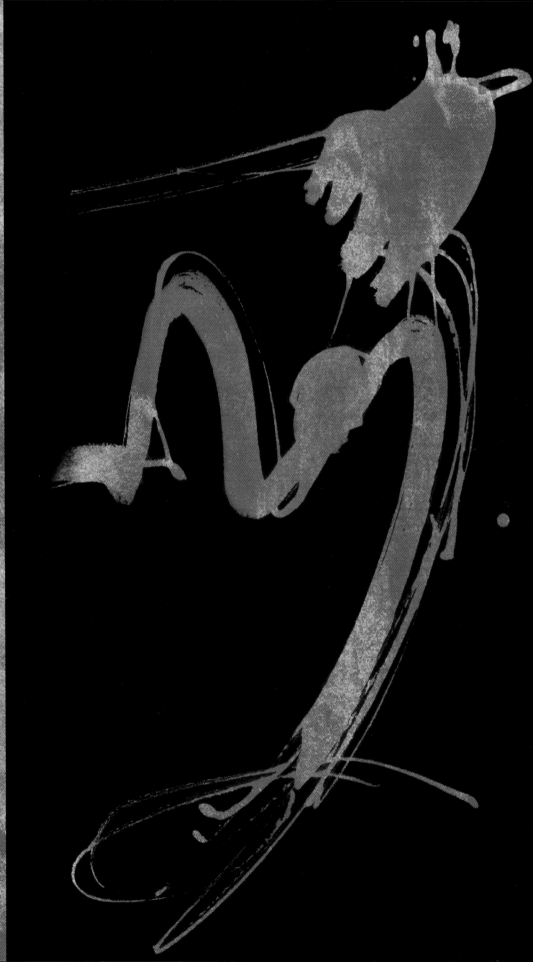

Outside I can hear the fireworks
Beyond the paper walls
Where the symbols painted black and white
Run together when the rain falls.
And the wind chimes across Kyoto
Each time the earth moves,
Was it the quake that shook me
Or was it something to do with you?

And the hot wind heats the bamboo blinds
And your almond eyes always shine
Sitting cool behind your painted fan
All the secrets of the east
Conceal the beauty and the beast
For tender is the man in her Japanese hands.

Flesh on silk looks different
Than on a cotton sheet back home
Where no one wears their hair like yours
Beneath those oriental combs
And with your thirsty fingers
Running up and down my spine
You forget the western woman
When you're sleeping on Kyoto time.

And the hot wind heats the bamboo blinds
And your almond eyes always shine
Sitting cool behind your painted fan
All the secrets of the east
Conceal the beauty and the beast
For tender is the man in her Japanese hands.

And the sky explodes
And the moon grows old
To the distant sound of drums
And the sky explodes
And the moon grows cold
As the dragons on the mainland
Wait to heat the sun.

just like belgium
»»»»»»

Remember Belgium and the Brussels Museum
Where we piled on the front steps like stray cavaliers
Our code of living meant little to others
The few francs we saved bought some cheap souvenirs

But the red lights where the catfights make it just like Belgium
See us face down on the floor of another cheap barroom
Streetwalkers sweet talk you out of your spare change
And your sweet madame makes it seem just like Belgium

Just like a hustler when they look attractive
It's nothing much more than a slap on the back
The price tag of being just a little bit different
The first rule to learn is to keep your own distance

just like strange rain

On my glass into the sky
There's no one in my comic book to buy
Calendars hung on the wall held by a rusty nail
Then down came the strange rain and washed my thoughts away

Look up in the sky and tell me why
You're changing the colours before my eyes
Yellow blue green and blue
Settling on the window pane

And then the rain that came seemed strange
Just like the strange rain
And then the rain it seemed strange
Just like strange rain

Still I sat beside the fire and watched it as it fell
Running colours from above into my citadel
My eyes are all embroidered with the rainbows you have made
And now it seems just like strange rain

Look up in the sky and tell me why
You're changing the colours before my eyes
Yellow blue green and blue
Settling on the window pane

And then the rain that came seemed strange
Just like the strange rain
And then the rain it seemed strange
Just like strange rain

kiss the bride

Well she looked a peach
In the dress she made
When she was still
Her mama's little girl
And when she walked down the aisle,
Everybody smiled
At her innocence and curls
And when the preacher said
'Is there anyone here
Gotta reason why they shouldn't wed?'
I should have stuck up my hand,
I should have got up to stand
And this is what I should have said

I wanna kiss the bride, yea!
I wanna kiss the bride, yea!
Long before she met him
She was mine, mine, mine
Don't say 'I do' say 'bye, bye, bye'
And let me kiss the bride, yea!

Underneath her veil I could see
A tear trickling down her pretty face
And when she slipped on the ring,
I knew everything would
Never be the same again
But if the groom would have known
He'd have had a fit
About his wife and the things we did
And what I planned to say,
Yea on her wedding day
Well I thought it but I kept it hid

lady samantha

When the shrill winds are screaming, and the
evening is still,
Lady Samantha glides over the hill
In a long satin dress that she wears every day;
Her home is the hillside, her bed is the grave.

Lady Samantha glides like a tiger
Over the hills with no one beside her,
No one comes near,
They all live in fear,
But Lady Samantha, she sheds only tears.

The tales that are told round the fire every night
Are out of proportion, and none of them right;
She is harmless and empty of anything bad,
For she once had something that most of you have.

lady what's tomorrow

Look up little brother
Can you see the clover
No, not over there, a little bit left
And over there

Now look and see the lilac tree
The lily pond, the skylark's song
The open air, but no one cares
If branches live and die out there

Remember when you were nine
And I was ten
We would run into the woods
No we never will again

And Lady, what's tomorrow
What's tomorrow anyway
If it's not the same as now
It's the same as yesterday

Yes Lady, what's tomorrow
Will it be the same as now
Will the farmer push the pen
Will the writer pull the plough

Look up little brother
Can you see the clover
Oh sorry, but it's over
Now there's concrete and no clover

latitude

Grey London morning
Wet London streets
Rain on the window
Wind in the trees
It's my time to write
It's your time to call

There's something about distance
That gets to us all

Dark clouds above me
Little people below
All walk with a purpose
With someplace to go
It's my place to paint
My own selfish scene
On this cold lonely canvass
It's just the weather and me

And latitude
Fold back the morning and bring on the night
There's an alien moon
That hangs between darkness and light
And latitude
Between me and you
You're a straight line of distance
A cold stretch of black across blue
Latitude

Cracks in the sidewalk
Dogs on the run
An old poster reading
'Give us your sons'
Window frames capture
Moments in time
But latitude captures
The heart and the mind

And latitude
Fold back the morning and bring on the night
There's an alien moon
That hangs between darkness and light
And latitude
Between me and you
You're a straight line of distance
A cold stretch of black across blue
Latitude

leather jackets

Do you pray to someone new
When you're locked up in the rock?
Is the golden age dead and gone
Are the hands stuck on the clock?
Can you talk to Buddy's bones
When you spin a forty-five
The king ain't dead, he's just asleep
Somewhere in the after life

And look at them boys in leather jackets
Second skin, not fade away
Danger girls love leather jackets
Play back to back, and that'll be the day
Leather jackets, that'll be the day

We all need to smell the heat
You know that things go better with chrome
Is Memphis real or just a song
Three thousand miles from home
Be a cool jerk, don't work
When fashion makes you change
Keep the faith, don't waste
Another nickel on another name

And look at them boys in leather jackets
Second skin, not fade away
Danger girls love leather jackets
Play back to back, and that'll be the day
Leather jackets, that'll be the day

And idolise twisted cars
Like taxi-cabs and spiders
Eternity's just down the road
They're looking for more riders

let me be your car

I may not seem your ideal when you look into my eyes,
I don't smoke, I don't tell jokes, I'm not the custom-made size:
But baby, let me take you on the highway for a while,
I'll show you where the man in me is when he doesn't hide,
He's cruisin' in the fast lane,
Stuck behind the wheel,
Jekyll and Hyde going on inside
When I'm your automobile.

And let me be your car for a while, child,
Shift me into gear and I'll be there,
Fill me up with five-star gasoline,
I'll be your car, I'll take you anywhere.

I can't dance, I don't dig it, I can't see it at all,
You say I'm just a specimen, and baby, I can crawl,
My physique don't look the way physiques really should,
But then again I've got an engine underneath my hood.
When I'm cutting up on the road
With a sports car on my tail,
Frankenstein's inside my mind
And the wind's inside my sails.

levon

Levon wears his war wound like a crown
He calls his child Jesus 'cause he likes the name
And he sends him to the finest school in town.

Levon, Levon likes his money
He makes a lot they say
Spends his days counting
In a garage by the motorway.

He was born a pauper
To a pawn on a Christmas day
When the New York Times
Said God is dead and war's begun.
Alvin Tostig has a son today.

And he shall be Levon
And he shall be a good man.
And he shall be Levon.
In tradition with the family plan
And he shall be Levon.
And he shall be a good man.
He shall be Levon.

Levon sells cartoon balloons in town.
His family business thrives.
Jesus blows up balloons all day,
Sits on the porch swing watching them fly.
And Jesus, he wants to go to Venus.
Leave Levon far behind.
Take a balloon and go sailing,
While Levon, Levon slowly dies.

And he shall be Levon.
And he shall be a good man.
He shall be Levon.

lies

Some lie about who they love
Some lie about the truth
Some lie to save their lives
Some lie about their youth
Some lie about age and beauty
And the conquest of sex
Most lie about about the night before
A woman lies for a party dress

I've lied for a stolen moment
I've lied for one more clue
I've lied about most everything
But I never lied to you

And we lie, lie, lie
On a streetcar named desire
Oh we lie, lie, lie
For that sweet bird of youth
I could be great like Tennessee Williams
If I could only hear something
That sounds like the truth

Some lie in the face of death
Some lie about their fame
Some kneel and lie to God
Some lie about their name
Some lie in words and speeches
With every living breath
The young lie with their guitars
The old lie for a little respect

I've lied to lie with danger
I've lied for a drug or two
I've lied about most everything
But I've never lied to you

And we lie, lie, lie
On a streetcar named desire
Oh we lie, lie, lie
For that sweet bird of youth
I could be great like Tennessee Williams
If I could only hear something
That sounds like the truth

I've lied for one more clue
I've lied about most everything
But I never lied to you

l'il 'frigerator

She looked so easy
'Cause she looked so young
With a geisha smile
Made in Taiwan
She got cherry bombs
Inside her eyes
And the luck of the Irish
On her side

Don't let her tell you
That she loves your mind
She's got her price
She can turn on a dime
Those crocodile tears
Ain't tears of pain
Look a little closer
That's acid rain

And I don't know
Why li'l 'frigerator you're so cold
Go li'l 'frigerator go
Get away from my soul
Li'l 'frigerator you're so cold

She's calculated
With the kiss of death
Got a digital mind
And expensive breath
She's an empty shell
You're a piece of meat
Just another statistic
On her readout sheet

lord of the flies

Well he looks through the wreckage
But he can't find a photo of you
Then he ties me in knots
With riddles he chooses to use

And he says how come you two
Are the only ones here who survived
I thought it was me
Who was destined to be
The lord of the flies

And who rules when fools leave
I do says the lord of the flies
Leave me your world, give me your earth
Swallow your foolish pride
And don't think I'm wrong
It's here I belong
It's mine, I'm the lord of the flies

Take all the money you want
It's the last thing we used for fuel
Here in the late great capital
We burned a bonfire for you

He knows we burnt the harvest
And saw through his disguise
He's no phantom at all
He's the only thing left
The lord of the flies

love is a cannibal

We follow the dog who follows the cat
And we swallow the chain if they don't fight back
We got a flag on the moon
We got a hole in the sky.

And each man kills the thing he loves
It's an edible romance we all dream of.

And love eats love, eats love
Love is a cannibal
Woman is a criminal
She have the hunger
But man is the animal
And love, eat love, eat love
Love is a cannibal.

We live in the woods but we hate the trees
We kill off the jungle but we save the leaves
The family face is painted grey
They did it for the baby and the wedding day.

And each man kills the thing he loves
It's an edible romance we all dream of.

And love eats love, eats love
Love is a cannibal
Woman is a criminal
She have the hunger
But man is the animal
And love, eat love, eat love
Love is a cannibal.

We follow the dog who follows the cat
And we swallow the chain if they don't fight back
We live in the woods but we hate the trees
We kill off the jungle but we save the leaves.

And each man kills the thing he loves
It's an edible romance we all dream of.

And love eats love, eats love
Love is a cannibal
Woman is a criminal
She have the hunger
But man is the animal
And love, eat love, eat love
Love is a cannibal.

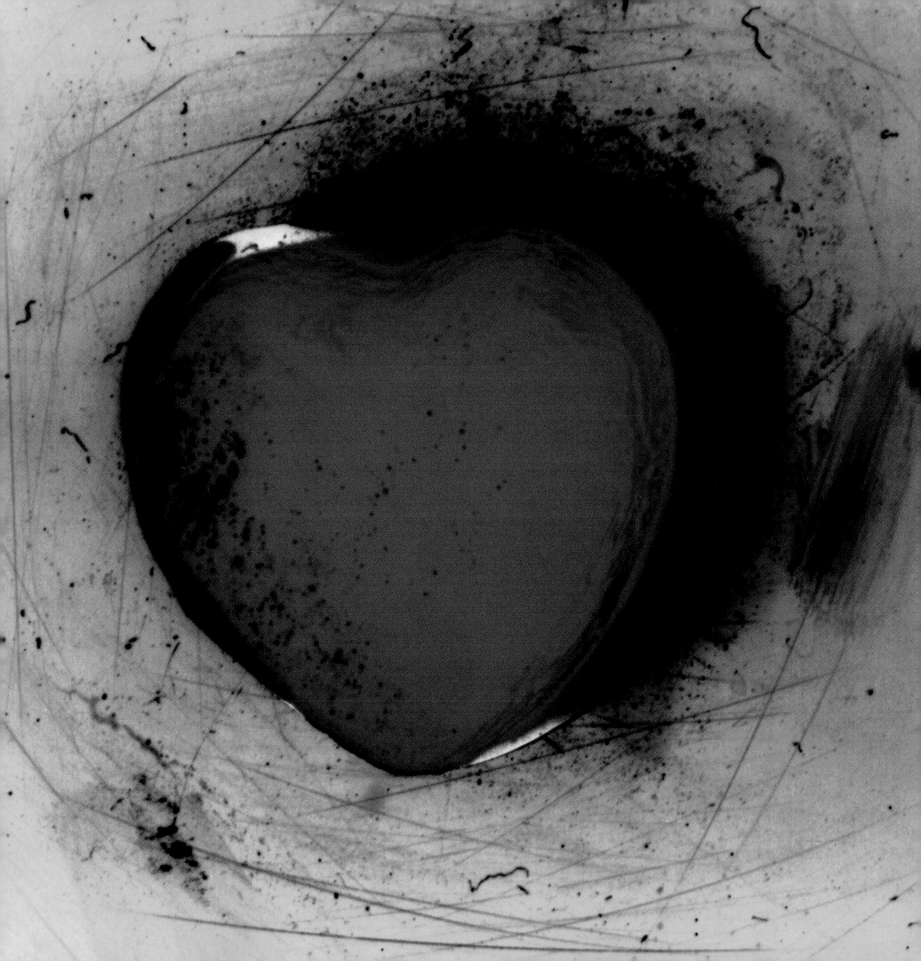

love lies bleeding

The roses in the window box
Have tilted to one side,
Everything about this house
Was born to grow and die.

It doesn't seem a year ago
To this very day
You said I'm sorry honey,
If I don't change the pace,
I can't face another day.

And love lies bleeding in my hand,
It kills me to think of you with another man.
I was playing rock 'n' roll and you were just a fan,
But my guitar couldn't hold you
So I split the band.
Love lies bleeding in my hands.

I wonder if those changes
Have left a scar on you,
Like all the burning hoops of fire
That you and I passed through.

You're a bluebird on a telegraph line
I hope you're happy now,
Well if the wind of change comes down your way girl
You'll make it back somehow.

lovesick

I've been blown away like a printed page that makes you lovesick
Headline news had me so abused but I was lovesick
You never tried although I sacrificed my weaknesses for you
I could have understood I should have read your looks
I should have gone mad at you I've been holding out
But it's time to shout you know I'm lovesick

I need a helping hand for a dying man who is so lovesick
I can't explain why I'll never change this thing grows deep inside
I've had doctors down and nurses round I've heard too many lies
You never tried and all I did was sacrifice
My weaknesses for you

I could have understood I could have read your looks
I should matter too I've been holding out
But it's time to shout you know I'm lovesick
A helping hand for a dying man who shows he's lovesick
I can't explain I'll never change this sickness deep inside

love so cold

It looked a lot like the same old thing
I've seen so many times
She was ageing fast
Like a man who's doing a life of crime
Meanwhile he held his crown and watched her tall
Just bouncing her around like a rubber ball

Through her washed out eyes
You could see the tides on her face had gone
She turned the radio off when she heard
What they had once called their song

And the crystal game they played
But the dream got more
And when they stayed out late
She knew what they stayed out for
Well love's so cold when you're growing old
And your looks are gone
Well love's so cold when you want to dance
But you can't for long
When you're sitting there at the red light
And the others go on
Love's so cold when you send out for your heart

Due to natural causes she became despondent
And she tried to leave
Bu the woman team had an SR2 up their sleeve
For he knew that a rage wouldn't help her get along
And that's what made his hold on her so strong
Well love's so cold when you're growing old
And your looks are gone
Well love's so cold when you want to dance
But you can't for long
When you're sitting there at the red light
And the others go on
Love's so cold when you send out for your heart

made for me

If I wasn't born to love you
Why was I born at all
If I wasn't made to hold you
What are these two arms for.

If I can't protect you
What are these muscles for
If I can't enrich your life
I might as well be poor.

If I couldn't see you naked
Oh I might as well be blind
If I couldn't treat you right
Wouldn't I be so unkind.

And you were made for me
You were made for me
You weren't born to be alone
No you were made for me.

Yea you were made for me
You were made for me
Flesh and bone, it's etched in stone
That you were made for me.

If I couldn't translate fantasy
Oh imagine how I'd feel
If I couldn't hear your secrets
My ears would both be sealed.

If I can't make love to you
This body has no use
If you believed I loved you
You wouldn't need no proof.

And if I can't return to you
I wouldn't need legs to run
And if I can't feel warmth from you
Then why do I need this sun.

made in england

I was made in England
Out of Cadillac muscle
I had a quit-me father
I had a love-me mother
I had Little Richard
And that black piano
Oh that sweet Georgia Peach
And the boy from Tupelo –

Wow oh oh oh I was made in England
Wow oh oh oh I was made in England

I was made in England
Out of Cadillac muscle
Face down on a playground
Crying God send me a brother
Not a bloody nose
For rock-'n'-roll
Give me that sweet Georgian Peach
And the boy from Tupelo

Wow oh oh oh I was made in England
Wow oh oh oh I was made in England

I was made in England
Like a blue Cortina
But a Yankee summer
Had a way about her
You had a scent for scandal
Well here's my middle finger
I had forty years of pain
And nothing to cling to

Wow oh oh oh I was made in England
Wow oh oh oh I was made in England

If you're made in England
You're built to last
You can still say homo
And everybody laughs
But the joke's on you
You never read the song
They all think they know
But they've all got it wrong –

Wow oh oh oh I was made in England
Wow oh oh oh I was made in England

madman across the water

I can see very well.
There's a boat on the reef with a broken back
And I can see it very well.
There's a joke and I know it very well,
It's one of those that I told you long ago.
Take my word I'm a madman don't you know.

Once a fool had a good part in the play,
If it's so would I still be here today?
It's quite peculiar in a funny sort of way,
they think it's very funny everything I say.
Get a load of him, he's so insane
You'd better get your coat dear
It looks like rain.

We'll come again next Thursday afternoon.
The in-laws hope they'll see you very soon.
But is it in your conscience that you're after
Another glimpse of the Madman across the Water.

I can see very well.
There's a boat on the reef with a broken back
And I can see it very well.
There's a joke and I know it very well,
It's one of those that I told you long ago.
Take my word I'm a madman don't you know.

We'll come again next Thursday afternoon.
The in-laws hope they'll see you very soon.
But is it in your conscience that you're after
Another glimpse of the Madman across the Water?

The ground's a long way down but I need more.
Is the nightmare black or are the windows painted?
Will they come again next week?
Can my mind really take it?

man

Man stands in all his glory
Sitting at the crossroads of the same old story
Man got his make-up wears it like a mask
Hides inside a child lives inside a glass
Man breathes his own deceit
Man worships his own defeat

I'm a man
I know what it feels like
I'm a man working on the living part of life
You see through me
I understand
Don't lose hope
If you can
Have a little faith in man

Shakespeare's men got all the lines
Modern man lives back in time
Man got bravado in his big steel hand
Runs with the wolf sleeps with the lamb
Man falls cuts and bleeds
Man stumbles on his own belief

I'm a man
I know what it feels like
I'm a man working on the living part of life
You understand
Don't lose hope
If you can
Have a little faith in man

He's the hoax
Behind the thrill
The poison arrow
The bitter pill
Hard to swallow
Hard to kill
Hard to understand
He's the light
Behind the hill
The broken promise
The iron will
Hard to kill
Hard to understand

Oh I'm a man
I know what it feels like
I'm a man working on the living part of life
You see through me
I understand
Don't lose hope
If you can
have a little faith in man
I know what it feels like
I'm a man working on the living part of life
You see through me
I understand
Don't lose hope
If you can
Have a little faith in man

Have a little faith in man

medicine man

We look at the table
And we look at the time
We see a short fuse burn
We're standin on the lime line

The look of the coldsuit
I look at the grey wall
I see a red flag burn
Yeah now we need a Santa Claus

Down on the haven
There's an avenue
Down among the rocky zone
Cradle falls but the bus stops here
Lets think about their hearts and bones

And call me I'll need a medicine man
I'll need a medicine man
Don't we need a medicine man
His shake and his rattle and his broken hand yeah yeah

See the mirrorness
On the back of a truck
I think we're wastin a dumb star
Hey sorry kid its Dublin

She was a dull boy
And he was a good boy
They were inseparable
Yeah bit him by the cold boy

Rack zone and shake the merry o
Tears among the cuts and blows
The backbone snaps and the kids come bats
They sing about their hearts and bones

And call me I'll need a medicine man
I'll need a medicine
don't we need a medicine man
His shake and his rattle and his broken hand yeah yeah

I'll need a medicine man
I'll need a medicine man
Don't we need a medicine man
Don't we need a helping hand
His shake and his rattle and his broken hand

medley (yell help, wednesday night, ugly)

Yell help,
Too many cooks and a bird in the bush.
Yell help.
Yell help,
If your mirror busts and your cat gets cussed
Yell help.
'Cause down the road you find someone else who's lookin',
Down the road you find another sweet lady cookin'
So I gotta yell help.
Yell help, yell help, yell help, yell help.
Some shelter from the storm like the travel agent warned
Yell help,
If you can help, your superstitions they gonna keep you warm
'Cause down the road you find someone else who's lookin',
Down the road you seen another sweet lady cookin'
So I gotta yell help,
Yell help, yell help, yell help, yell help, yell help.

I wish tonight wasn't Wednesday night,
And I wish it wasn't the thirteenth of July.
And you're looking at the guy whose eyes can't deny
That he wishes he were somewhere else tonight.

Well, I met this woman down in New Orleans.
Lord, she built just like a dream
Even wore stockings that had seams,
And she was ugly.

Now hell, I don't mind
Women of her kind
I'll even pay sometimes for a woman that's ugly.

She built like a steamroller,
Just the kind to mow you over, anytime
The moment might arrive.

On Bourbon Street
Well the ugliest women you'll ever meet,
But she mine my my mine and she's ugly.

mellow

Cool grass blowin' up the pass,
don't you know I'm feeling mellow.
I love your Roman nose,
the way you curl your toes,
Baby, makes me feel so mellow.

It's the same old feeling I get
when you're stealin' back into my bed again,
With the curtains closed and the window froze
By the rhythm of the rain.

You make me mellow, you make me mellow,
Rockin' smooth and slow,
Mellow's the feeling that we get
Watchin' the coal fire glow.

You make me mellow, I make you mellow,
Wreckin' the sheets real fine,
Heaven knows what you sent me Lord.
But God this is a mellow time.

Going down to the stores in town
gettin' all the things we need,
Don't forget the beer, my little dear,
It helps to sow the mellow seed.

And it can't be bad,
All the love I've had
Coursin' through my life,
Down in the pass
Where the wind blows fast
And mellow's a feelin' right.

michelle's song

Cast a pebble on the water,
Watch the ripples gently spreading,
Tiny daughter of the Camargue,
We were meant to be together.
We were made for one another
In a time it takes to grow up,
If only we were old enough
Then they might leave us both alone.

So take my hand in your hand,
Say it's great to be alive,
No one's going to find us
No matter how they try,
No one's going to find us,
It's wonderful so wild beneath the sky.

Sleeping in the open,
See the shadows softly moving,
Take a train towards the southlands,
Our time was never better.
We shall pass such sights of splendour
On the door of a new life,
It had to happen soon I guess,
Whether it is wrong or it is right.

We learned to be so graceful
Watching wild horses running,
And from those agile angels
We knew the tide was turning.
For we watched as on the skyway
The herons circled slowly,
While we mere mortals watched them fly
Our sleepless eyes grew heavy.

midnight creeper

Walk a mile in my tennis shoes,
Tina Turner gave me the highway blues,
But I don't love nobody but you, honey.

I'm true rat for the things I done,
Second cousin to a son of a gun,
I'm gonna wipe out your mama if she puts me on, honey.

'Cause I'm a midnight creeper,
Ain't gonna lose no sleep over you,
When there's a nightmare, I'm there,
Tempting you to blow a fuse.

Well there's no more sleepin'
When I'm midnight creepin' over you,
Watch out honey, watch out honey,
Watch the things you do.

Long-haired ladies well they look at me,
Locked in my cellar full of cheap red wine,
But, I don't think those ladies they really mind, honey.

I still don't know why you hate me so,
A little bit of fun never stopped no show,
Well I just want to loosen up my soul, honey.

mona lisas and mad hatters

And now I know, Spanish Harlem
Are not just pretty words to say.
I thought I knew,
But now I know that rose trees never grow in New York city.

Until you've seen this trash-can dream come true,
You stand at the edge while people run you through
And I thank the Lord there's people out there like you.

While Mona Lisas and Mad Hatters,
Sons of bankers, sons of lawyers,
Turn around and say good morning to the night,
For unless they see the sky,
But they can't, and that is why
They know not if it's dark outside or light.

This Broadway's got a lot of songs to sing,
If I knew the tunes, I might join in.
I'll go my way alone,
Grow my own, my own seeds shall be sown in New York city.

Subway's no way for a good man to go down,
Rich man can ride, and the hobo he can drown,
And I thank the Lord for the people I have found.

IF YOU CUT THE PAGES AS INDICATED YOU
WILL BE ABLE TO MAKE SOME AMUSING PICTURES

mona lisas and mad hatters (part two)

I used to think that New York City
Fell from grace with God
And innocence abroad
Waged a war for the underdog
When the snow falls
And Central Park looks like a Christmas card
I Just looked beyond the bagman
And the madness that makes this city hard.

I heard a basketball
Somewhere out beyond a chainlink fence
Inner city prisoners
Argue for the right of self-defense
But there's a fast break
And every work of art wakes something in the soul
Just focus on the brush strokes
And the bouquets that the dancers hold.

Spanish Harlem still sounds good to me
Yeah Mona Lisa's getting older
Standing in the shadow of Miss Liberty
While I walk along the west side
Down through Little Italy
Searching for the city that
That took away the kid in me.

my father's gun

From this day on I own my father's gun
We dug his shallow grave beneath the sun
I laid his broken body down below the southern land
It wouldn't do to bury him where any Yankee stands

I'll take my horse and I'll ride the northern plain
To wear the colour of the greys and join the fight again
Oh I'll not rest until I know the cause is fought and won
From this day on until I die I'll wear my father's gun

I'd like to know where the riverboat sails tonight
To New Orleans well that's just fine, alright
'Cause there's fighting there and the company needs men
So slip us a rope and sail on round the bend

As soon as this is over we'll go home
To plant the seeds of justice in our bones
To watch the children growing and see the women sewing
There'll be laughter when the bells of freedom ring.

nikita

Hey Nikita is it cold
In your little corner of the world
You could roll around the globe
And never find a warmer soul to know

Oh I saw you by the wall
Ten of your tin soldiers in a row
With eyes that looked like ice on fire
The human heart a captive in the snow

Oh Nikita you will never know anything about my home
I'll never know how good it feels to hold you
Nikita I need you so
Oh Nikita is the other side of any given line in time
Counting ten tin soldiers in a row
Oh no, Nikita you'll never know

Do you ever dream of me
Do you ever see the letters that I write
When you look up through the wire
Nikita do you count the stars at night

And if there comes a time
Guns and gates no longer hold you in
And if you're free to make a choice
Just look towards the west and find a friend

Oh Nikita you will never know, anything about my home
I'll never know how good it feels to hold you
Nikita I need you so
Oh Nikita is the other side of any given line in time
Counting ten tin soldiers in a row
Oh no, Nikita you'll never know

no shoestrings on louise

Lady love rides a big red Cadillac
Buys the hoedown show salt and beans
Goes to the church to pray for Lucifer
She milked the male population clean.

So ride in the line shake yourself by the hand
Live your life inside a paper can
But you'll never get to pick and choose
She's bought you and sold you
There ain't no shoestrings on Louise.

Come on down, come on down from the ladder
Henry get your head out of the clouds
What she wants is to go kissing on a swine herd
You might as well kiss the boss man's cow.

All those city women want to make us poor men
And this land's got the worse for the worrying
I got married at the early age of fourteen
And I've been worrying about the way you'll be loving 'em.

on dark street

I'm staring down a mile of disappearing track
Is this best that we could do
I'm leaning through the rain but you ain't looking back
What did I ever have to prove?

'Cause it feels like electricity hitting an open field
When am I ever gonna learn?
Married life's two people trying to grab the wheel

Oh and we must have got lost
Livin' on Dark Street
Lookin' for an exit
Sleepin' on the concrete
You can't see it with your eyes
You can't find it with your feet
All I know is that we're lost baby
And we're livin' on Dark Street

All the layoffs and the pay cuts cripple me inside
I pay the price for living every day
Trying to keep us all together along with a little pride
Umm what'll it take to make you stay

But I've dreamed about an island all I got's a bucket of sand
I'd give my eyes to give you all your dreams
Now I get to see my family slipping through my hands

You can't see it with your eyes
You can't find it with your feet
All I know is that we're lost baby
And we're livin' on Dark Street
Oh yeah

one horse town

Saw a Cadillac for the first time yesterday.
I'd always seen horses, buggies, bales of hay.
'Cause progress here don't move with modern times.
There's nothing to steal.
So there's not a great deal of crime.

Sure is hell living in a one horse town,
Half a mile of Alabama mud bed ground.
Nothing much doing of an afternoon,
Unless you're sitting in a rocking chair just picking a tune.

And they ain't too well acquainted with the Stars and Stripes
But if you wanna hear Susanna then they'll pick all night
They'll pick all night.

'Cause it's no dice living in a one horse town,
Laid back, as my old coon hound.
And I just can't wait to get out of this one horse town,
There's nothing to steal 'cause there's nothing much around.

Sure is hell living in this one horse town,
Half a mile of Alabama mud bed ground.
And I just can't wait to grow out of this one horse town,
There's nothing to steal 'cause there's nothing much around.

one more arrow

He said I want to grow up
And look like Robert Mitchum
And I hope that when I'm gone
There'll be some say that I miss him
He must have been romantic
He must have sensed adventure
And I feel the steel of his strong will
In the frame around his picture

And he's one more arrow,
Flying through the air
One more arrow landing in
A shady spot somewhere
Where the days and nights

Blend into one
And he can always feel the sun
Through the soft brown earth
That holds him forever always young

He could have been a boxer
But the fight game seemed so dirty
We argued once he knocked me down
And he cried when he thought
He'd hurt me
Strictly from the old school
He was quiet about his pain
And if one in ten could be that brave
I would never hate again

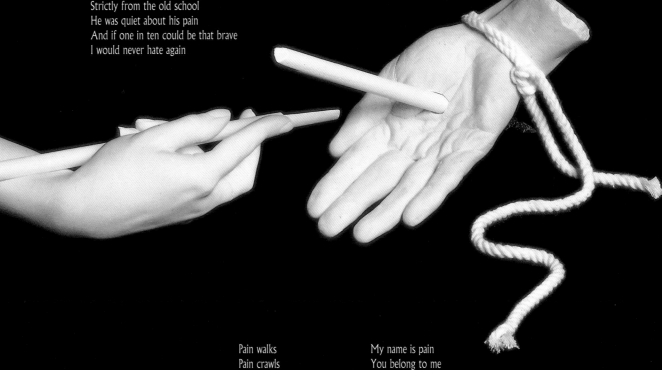

pain

What's your name?
My name is pain
Where do you live?
I live anyplace
Where were you born?
In the state of fear
How old are you?
Nineteen hundred
and ninety-four years

What's your plan?
My plan is pain
When will you leave?

I'll never go away
How will you breathe?
You'll give me life
How will you see?
Sitting in the temple
Right between your eyes

My name is pain
You belong to me
You're all I ever wanted
I'm all you'll ever be

From the beginning
In a World without end
I am the air
I am pain

Pain is love
Pain is pure
Pain is sickness
Pain is the cure
Pain is death
Pain is the religion
Pain is life
Pain is television

Pain walks
Pain crawls
Pain is peace
Pain is war

Where were you born
In the state of fear
How old are you?
Nineteen hundred
and ninety-four years

My name is pain
You belong to me
You're all I ever wanted
I'm all you'll ever be

My name is pain
You belong to me
You're all I ever wanted
I'm all you'll ever wanted
I'm all you'll ever be

From the beginning
In a World without end
I am the air
I am pain

From the beginning
In a World without end
I am the air
I am pain

paris

Nobody left in the airport lounge
They cleaned the ashtrays
TV's just wound down
I've gotta wait til morning
I've gotta last the night
I've only got one book
To see me through my flight

But when I get to Paris
We'll paint all our portraits
In brushstrokes of yellow
And christen the canvas
The Left Bank is crying
For colour to crown it
Like the roof of a palace
We'll drink in the amber
When I get to Paris

You were the best of Montmartre street life
You signed the tablecloth
Art has its price
It's so hard to hold on
To the ghost of your breed
It takes ambition
To call the colours you need

But when I get to Paris
We'll paint all our portraits
In brushstrokes of yellow
And christen the canvas
The Left Bank is crying
For colour to crown it
Like the roof of a palace
We'll drink in the amber
When I get to Paris

I've gotta wait till morning
I've gotta last the night
I've only got one book
To see me through my flight

Like the roof of a palace
We'll drink in the amber
When I get to Paris

passengers

Deny the passenger, who wanna get on
Deny the passenger, who wanna get on
Deny the passenger, who wanna get on
Wanna get on, wanna get on
He wanna get on, he wanna get on
Wanna get on, wanna get on
He wanna get on, he wanna get on

To make a chain of fools
You need a matching pair
One hypocritical fool
And a crowd that's never there
There's anger in the silence
There's wheels upon the jail
A black train built of bones
On a copper rail

Company conductor
You need the salt of tears
Falling on a ticket
That no-one's used in years
Non commercial native
It's tattooed in your veins
You're living in a blood bank
And riding on this train

The spirit's free, but you always find
Passengers stand and wait in line
Someone in the front and someone behind
But passengers always wait in line

philadelphia freedom

I used to be a rolling stone
You know if the cause was right
I'd leave to find the answer on the road.
I used to be a heart beating for someone
But the times have changed
The less I say the more my work gets done.

'Cause I live and breathe this Philadelphia Freedom
From the day that I was born I've waved the flag
Philadelphia Freedom took me knee-high to a man
Yeah! gave me peace of mind my daddy never had.
Oh Philadelphia Freedom shine on me, I love you
Shine a light through the eyes of the ones left behind
Shine a light shine a light
Shine a light won't you shine a light
Philadelphia Freedom I love you, yes I do.

If you choose to you can live your life alone
Some people choose the city,
Some others choose the good old family home
I like living easy without family ties
'Til the whippoorwill of freedom zapped me
Right between the eyes.

pinky

I don't want to wake you
But I'd like to tell you that I love you
That the candlelight fell like a crescent upon your feather pillow.

For there's more ways than one
And the ways of the world are a blessing
For when Pinky's dreamin'
She owes the world nothing
And her silence keeps us guessing.

Pinky's as perfect as the Fourth of July
Quilted and timeless
Seldom denied
The trial and the error of my masterplan
Now she rolls like the dice
In a poor gambler's hands.

You don't want to tell me
But somehow you've guessed that I know
Oh, when dawn came this morning
You discovered a feeling that burned like a flame in your soul.

For there's toast and honey
And there's breakfast in bed on a tray
Oh, it's ten below zero
And we're about to abandon our plans for the day.

please

We've been crippled in love
Short changed and hung out to dry
We've chalked on the walls
A slogan or two about life
Stood dazed in the doorway
The king and queen of clowns
We've been flipped like a coin
Both of us landing face down

So please, please
Let me grow old with you
After everything we've been through
What's left to prove
So please, please, please, please
Let me grow old with you

We've been living with sorrow
Been up, down and all around
We've buried our feelings
A little too deep in the ground
Stood dazed in the doorway
The king and queen of clowns
We've been flipped like a coin
Both of us landing face down

So please, please
Let me grow old with you
After everything we've been through
What's left to prove
So please, please, please, please
Let me grow old with you

But tied to the same track
The two of us look back
At oncoming trains ahead
How many more times
Can we lay on the line
Watching our love hang by a thread

So please, please
Let me grow old with you
After everything we've been through
What's left to prove
So please, please, please, please
Please, please, please, please
Let me grow old with you

poor cow

There's another one due in three months time
She'll have to paint the spare room blue
She'll work a little overtime
And hope it all works out with Frank and her,
If she can keep him home nights
Away from those factory girls.

And the gas bills come and the money burns
And Frank just keeps complainin'
How little they both earn.
And mother drops by Mondays
Just to nag about the world
Then she stays to nag at Dallas
'Cause she hates those Texas girls.

Poor cow You'll get your dumb man
You'll see your whole life comin' at you
In the back of his hand.
Poor cow It's a monkey see town
You'll walk down the aisle
In the hand me down gown
Of some poor cow.

And the gas bills come and the money burns
And Frank just keeps complainin'
How little they both earn.
And mother drops by Mondays
Just to nag about the world
Then she stays to nag at Dallas
'Cause she hates those Texas girls.

Poor cow You'll get your dumb man
You'll see your whole life comin' at you
In the back of his hand
Poor cow
It's a monkey see town
You'll walk down the aisle
In the hand me down gown
Of some poor cow.

Oh them rich bitch girls
Ain't like our lass
Got no spine for labour
Like us working class.
Us gamey lot
Still got our pride
We got our health
It's just the truth that's died.

razor face

Has anybody here seen Razor Face.
Heard he's back, lookin' for a place, to lay down.
Must be getting on.
Needs a man who's young to walk him round,
Needs a man who's young to walk him round.

Oh it must be hard for the likes of you,
To get by in a world that you just can't see through
And it looks so cold.
How does it feel to know you can't go home,
How does it feel to know you can't go home.

Come on Razor Face my old friend,
I'll meet you down by the truck stop inn,
With a bottle of booze in the back of my car,
You're a song on the lips of an ageing star.

Razor Face, amazing grace,
Protects you like a glove.
And I'll never learn the reason why
I love your Razor Face.

religion

Well he could almost taste the money
But he was sitting in
A den of thieves
Looking for the great awakening
Trying to find a way to leave

But that's when he got religion
And the light went on inside
He said 'somebody up there likes me'
Now he's working for the holy guide

He got drunk but he don't remember
That he'd been drinking
In a bar downtown
When he thought he heard
A choir of angels
Singing in the 'Tiki Lounge'

And that's when he got religion
From no salesman on TV
Just a tap on the shoulder
In the parking lot
He still drinks but he does believe

Religion
Oh you do the best you can
We all make the same mistakes
We're gonna wind up with the man

She was silent as he paid her
But the thanks she got
Was next to none
And as her car pulled out of the motel
She felt the presence of someone

And that's when she got religion
In the front of a compact Ford
Just a gentle voice on the stereo
Now she's a workin' girl
Who loves the Lord

restless

It's a hot summer night in the blackboard jungle
Crime sits heavy on the city's shoulder
Can't get no work, I can't get a job
I just sit and play my radio in the parking lot

Well they're breaking down doors in foreign countries
Everybody thinks somebody's hiding something
There's talk on the street and the nation is worried
But you can't talk back when you're dead, when you're dead and buried

And everybody's restless
Everybody's scared
Everybody's looking for something, that just ain't there
Everybody's restless

Everybody's scared – they think we're all in danger
Everyone's taking cover from someone else's anger
The walls have ears, Big Brother's watching
They tell us that we're poisoned from everything that we're touching

Well we could be children from the way we're acting
We feed ourselves lies and then we scream for action
We just breed and we lose our nerve
And there're bombs going off in every corner of the world

rock 'n' roll madonna

If anyone should see me making it down the highway,
Breaking all the laws of the land,
Well, don't you try to stop me, I'm going her way,
And that's the way I'm sure she had it planned.

Well, that's my rock 'n' roll Madonna
She's always been a lady of the road;
Well, everybody wants her,
But no one ever gets her,
Well, the freeway is the only way she knows.

Well, if she would only slow down for a short while
I'd get to know her just before she leaves
But she's got some fascination for that two-wheel combination
And I swear it's going to be the death of me.

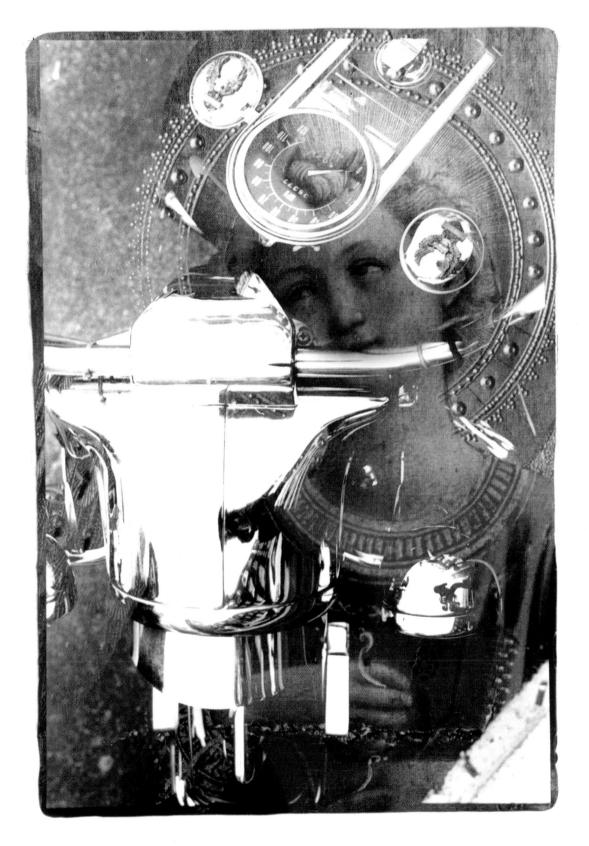

rocket man

She packed my bags last night
Pre-flight,
Zero hour, nine a.m.
And I'm gonna be high as a kite by then.

I miss the earth so much,
I miss my wife.
It's lonely out in space
On such a timeless flight.

And I think it's gonna be a long, long time
Till touchdown brings me round again to find
I'm not the man they think I am at home.
Oh, no, no, no,
I'm a rocket man,
Rocket man burning out his fuse up here alone.

Mars ain't the kind of place to raise your kids,
In fact it's cold as hell
And there's no one there to raise them if you did.

And all this science,
I don't understand.
It's just my job, five days a week,
A rocket man.

rope around a fool

I don't make the rules 'round here
A tear starts at the edge
It takes two hands to rip it
It takes a lot more than either one of us has said.

But I come from Indecision
A place you've never been
Living in the State of Confusion
On a map that runs like the veins under your skin.

We get Miss Communication, kicking out the stoll
We got mass determination, making up the rules
But saving us is something we can't do
Easier to throw a rope around a fool.

And love is just another means
By which we hang ourselves
It takes two to execute
One to leave with innocence and one to live with guilt.

And you see no reality
Just shades drawn on remorse
We've whipped this beast beyond its limit
Staggered out of breath along this course.

Bridge
And it's easier to lose
A rope around a fool
A ring of your indifference
Thrown any place you choose.

rotten peaches

We've moved on six miles from where we were yesterday
And yesterday is but a long long ways away.
So we'll camp out tonight beneath the bright starlight,
And forget rotten peaches and the places we've stayed.

I left from the dockland two years ago now
Made my way over on the S. S. Marie.
And I've always had trouble wherever I've settled
Rotten peaches are all that I see.

Rotten peaches, rotting in the sun
Seems I've seen that devil fruit, since the world begun.
Mercy I'm a criminal, Jesus I'm the one
Rotten peaches, rotting in the sun.

There ain't no green grass in the U.S. State prison
There is no one to hold when you're sick for your wife
And each day out you'll pick you'll pick rotten peaches.
You'll pick rotten peaches for the rest of your life.

Oh I've had me fill of cocaine and pills,
For I lie in the light of the Lord
And my home is ten thousand, ten thousand miles away
And I guess I won't see it no more.

Rotten peaches, rotting in the sun.
Seems I've seen that devil fruit, since the world begun.
Mercy I'm a criminal, Jesus I'm the one.
Rotten peaches, rotting in the sun.

roy rogers

Sometimes you dream,
Sometimes it seems
There's nothing there at all.
You just seem older
Than yesterday,
And you're waiting
For tomorrow to call.

You draw to the curtains,
And one thing's for certain
You're cozy in your little room
The carpet's all paid for,
God bless the T.V.
Let's shoot a hole in the moon.

And Roy Rogers is riding tonight,
Returning to our silver screens.
Comic book characters never grow old,
Evergreen heroes whose stories were told,
The great sequin cowboy
Who sings of the plains,
Of roundups and rustlers,
And home on the range,
Turn on the T. V.
Shut out the lights —
Roy Rogers is riding tonight.

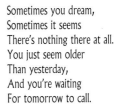

Nine o'clock mornings
Five o'clock evenings
I'd liven the pace if I could.
I'd rather have ham in my sandwich than cheese
But complaining wouldn't do any good.

Lay back in my armchair
Close eyes and think clear
I can hear hoofbeats ahead
Roy and Trigger have just hit the hilltop
While the wife and the kids are in bed.

runaway train

There's a hungry road I can only hope's
Gonna eat me up inside
There's a drifting spirit coming clean
In the eye of a lifelong fire
Tell Monday I'll be around next week
I'm running ahead of my days
In the shotgun chance that scattered us
I've seen the error of my ways

Oh, oh, oh, oh

Well we've wrapped ourselves in golden crowns
Like sun gods spitting rain
Found a way home written on this map
Like red dye in my veins
In the hardest times that come around
The fear of losing grows
I've lost and seen the world shut down
It's darkness no one knows

Oh, oh, oh, oh

And I've poured out the pleasure and dealt with the pain
Standing in a station waitin' in the rain
I'm starting to feel a little muscle again
But love is lost like a runaway train
Well I'm out of control and out of my hands
I'm tearing like a demon through no man's land
Trying to get a grip on my life again
Nothing hits harder than a runaway train

Oh, oh, oh, oh

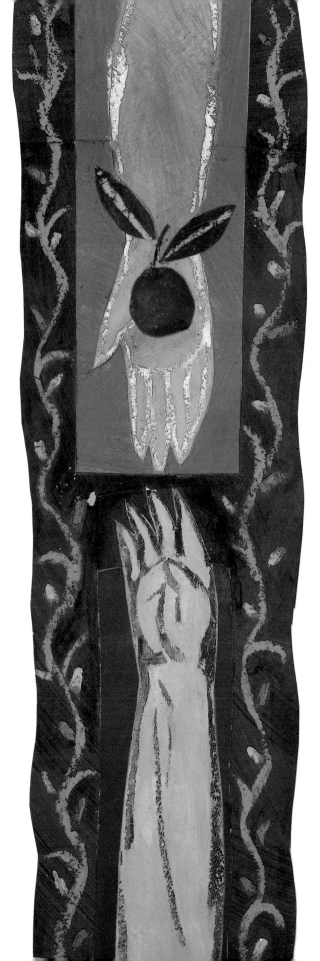

sacrifice

It's a human sign
When things go wrong
When the scent of her lingers
And temptations strong

In to the boundary
Of each married man
Sweet deceit comes a callin'
And negativity lands

Cold, cold heart
Hard done by you
Some things look better baby
Just passin' through

And it's no sacrifice
Just a simple word
It's two hearts living
In two separate worlds
But it's no sacrifice
No sacrifice
It's no sacrifice at all

Mutual misunderstanding
After the fact
Sensitivity builds a prison
In the final act

We loose direction
No stone unturned
No tears to damn you
When jealousy burns

Cold, cold heart
Hard done by you
Some things look better baby
Just passing through

And it's no sacrifice
Just a simple word
It's two hearts living
In two separate worlds
But it's no sacrifice
No sacrifice
It's no sacrifice at all

sad songs (say so much)

Guess there are times when we all need to share a little pain
And ironing out the rough spots
Is the hardest part when memories remain
And it's times like these when we all need to hear the radio
'Cause from the lips of some old singer
We share the troubles we already know

Turn 'em on, turn 'em on
Turn on those sad songs
When all hope is gone
Why don't you tune in and turn them on

They reach into your room
Just feel their gentle touch
When all hope is gone
Sad songs say so much

If someone else is suffering enough to write it down
When every single word makes sense
Then it's easier to have those songs around
The kick inside is in the line that finally gets to you
And it feels so good to hurt so bad
And suffer just enough to sing the blues

Sad songs they say, sad songs they say
Sad songs they say, sad songs they say so much

121

sails

I viewed in my presence
My hand on my forehead
And sighting the liners
Of mad merchant seamen
In search of the living
Or the spices of China

Lucy walked gently
Between the damp barrels
And shut out my eyes
With the width of her fingers
Said she'd guessed the number
Of bales in the back-room

While the seagulls were screaming
Lucy was eating
Then we hauled up our colours
The way the mother had told us
And together we just watched the sails

Lucy, I said
In a passage of cotton kegs
Can we hold hands
I'm sure that it's warmer
Then the gulls ate the crumbs
Of Lucy's sandwich

saint

You don't pass your time in limbo
Or hang out with the crowd
Sitting on the stoop
Like a little girl
Who took the wrong road into town
But you got that short cut way about you
And no one's gonna stare you down
You cook much better on a lower flame
You burn much better when
The sun goes down

And heaven can wait
But you ought to be a saint
I got your very best intentions
Helping me along
And if I ever fail to mention
You were an overnight sensation
Well take it from me,
My baby's a saint

I believe you were a new arrival
On the fast train passing through
And you traded in
Your luck for survival
To sweeten up the witches brew
You had a better way of working magic
A little mystery in your eyes
Instead of rolling over
You remained the same
You took the whole world by surprise

salvation

I have to say, my friends,
This road goes a long, long way,
And if we're going to find the end
We're gonna need a helping hand.

I have to say, my friends,
We're looking for a light ahead,
In the distance a candle burns,
Salvation keeps the hungry children fed.

It's gonna take a lot of salvation,
What we need are willing hands,
You must feel the sweat in your eyes,
You must understand, salvation.

A chance to put the devil down
Without the fear of hell.
Salvation spreads the gospel round,
And free you from yourself.

satellite

Well you come on like a comet
Ideas in your head
Starving for affection
Waiting to be fed

Crazy like a full moon
Eyes open wide
Taking in everything
You need to stay alive

Who leads who
Who knows when
If you leave me now
Will I see you again

I'm telling you
Love bites
Like a satellite
Going round and round
It's something, something you can't fight

Oh in the daylight
And even in the dark night
I want you to surround me
Surround me like a satellite

Oh you move like a shadow
Of your own design
Do you want to trap me
In between the lines

I don't walk on water
If you think I can
If you want a miracle
Call up a Superman

saturday night's alright for fighting

It's gettin' late have yer seen my mates,
Ma tell me when the boys get here,
It's seven o'clock and I want to rock
Wanna get a belly full of beer.

My old man's drunker than a barrel full of monkeys
And my old lady she don't care,
My sister looks cute in her braces and boots
A handful of grease in her hair.

So don't give us none of yer aggravation
We've had it with yer discipline,
Saturday night's alright for fightin',
Get a little action in.

Get about as oiled as a diesel train
Gonna set this dance alight,
'Cause Saturday night's the night I like
Saturday night's alright, alright, alright.

Well they're packed pretty tight in here tonight
I'm looking for a dolly who'll see me right,
I may use a little muscle to get what I need
I sink a little drink and shout out 'She's with me'.

A couple of the sounds that I really like
Are the sound of a switchblade and a motorbike,
I'm a juvenile product of the working class
Who's best friend floats in the bottom of a glass.

screw you

When I was a boy I had a lot of fun,
I lived by the sea, I was a fisherman's son;
My mother, she was a fisherman's wife,
She was scrubbing floors most of her life.

They said, Screw you,
I ain't got nothing to lose,
I could paper a matchbox with the money I use.

At the school I attended I got into fights,
I was beaten in an alley on a cold winter night;
The teachers cared less for the blood in our veins,
They got most of their thrills out of using the cane.

They said, Screw you,
Oh, you bloody young fools,
I could get more sense out of the back end of a mule.

So you see, there's men who get paid for being slaves,
And men who get paid for being free,
And there's men behind bars who pray for the light,
And men in the suburbs who pray for the night;
And they're all trying to climb to the top of the mine,
And all of them say most of the way,
Screw you.

I worked in the mill from seven till nine,
Tears in my eyes nearly drove me half-blind,
Trying to make wages that weren't even there,
Taking hell from a foreman with the build of a bear.

He said, Screw you,
This is all you'll ever do,
It's the only existence for someone like you.

seasons

For our world the circle turns again,
Throughout the year were seen the seasons change.
It's meant a lot to me to start anew,
Oh, the winter's cold and I'm so warm with you.

Out there there's not a sound to be heard,
And the seasons seem to sleep upon their words,
As the waters freeze up with the summer's end.
Oh, it's funny how young lovers start as friends,
Yes, it's funny how young lovers start as friends.

shoot down
the moon

Oh no I don't want it
You can take it all
I'll put my money where my mouth is
Put your suitcase in the hall

Oh you robbed me blind
Of what little hope remained
You put a gun to my head
A bullet through my brain

You can't shoot down the moon
Some things never change
We can build a bridge between us
But the empty space remains

Just as long as you're around
We live on borrowed time
I'll put my money where my mouth is
You're guilty at the scene of the crime

I never say more than I need
The mystery runs deep
The dangers buried below
The secrets that you keep

You can't shoot down the moon
Some things never change
We can build a bridge between us
But the empty space remains

shoulder holster

Now, it was just like Frankie and Johnny
And it was just like Stagger Lee
Dolly Summers was a simple girl
From a mid-west family.
With a stucco home and her own Mustang
And a charge account at Sears,
She had everything that a girl could want
To live happy for the rest of her years.

But the thing that she wanted most of all
Was the thing that she had lost
To the arms of a downtown blackjack hustler
By the name of Candyfloss.
They'd slipped town on a late night train
Heading for the West.
Dolly slipped behind the wheel of her Mustang
With a piece between her breast.

She put a pistol in her shoulder holster
She took her car up from Santa Fe
Yesterday morning she was washing dishes
Now she's hunting down a runaway.
Don't judge a man by a misdemeanour
You may be sorry when his light goes out
Don't put that pistol in your shoulder holster.

If it seems just like a movie
Or a night of bad T.V.
They should have had a picture of Dolly's face
As she drove across country.
With daggers drawn for her fallen man
And venom in her heart,
It was nearly dawn when she caught them up
Making out in a picnic park.

But the thing that shook her rigid
As she fumbled for her gun
Was the state of the man that she'd married once
And thought of as the only one.
And as she looked back on the chances
That she'd passed up at home,
Well, she quietly dumped her pistol in a ditch
And she headed home alone.

sick city

'Oooh,' she said,
'The crowd just loved you,
My name's Angel and I'm sixteen,
I really love your band,
And your funny accent,
Sure would like to cruise in your limousine.'

Then she said,
'How about a rubdown?
You're so cute and I'm so mean,
The way you hold your guitar really gets me,
I can show you tricks that you ain't never seen.'

Sick City,
Nobody to love you,
Oh but sometimes I can taste you when I'm feeling weak,
Sick City,
Isn't it a pity?
That you can't float above it when the bottom leaks,
Oh, oh, sick City.

'Hey man,
How's about a handout?
All you dudes just loaded down,
Just a little sugar man, makes me sweeter,
I like to sit at home and watch the world go round.'

Stage-door monkey's on my back,
Begging me to save his life,
Can't he understand we're not a healing show?
We're just here to play some music for the kids tonight.

simple life

There's a breakdown on the runway
And the timeless flights are gone
I'm a year ahead of myself these days
And I'm locomotive strong
My city spread like cannon fire
In a yellow nervous state
Can't cut the ties that bind me
To horoscopes and fate

And I won't break and I won't bend
But someday soon we'll sail away
To innocence and the bitter end
And I won't break and I won't bend
And with the last breath we ever take
We're gonna get back to the simple life again

When we break out of this blindfold
I'll take you from this place
Until we're free from this ball and chain
I'm still hard behind the eight
My city beats like hammered steel
On a shallow cruel rock
If we could walk proud after midnight
We'd never have to stop

since god invented girls

The mother of invention made it good for me
Tighter in the rear
Longer in the seam
Kicked out yards of leather
Wrapped around her waist
Trimmed it to perfection
And left a little space.

Yeah they got competition now
All across the world
But there ain't been no lookin' back
Since God invented girls.

Now I know what Brian Wilson meant
Every time I step outside
I see what Heaven sent
There may be seven wonders
Created for this world
But one is all we need
Since God invented girls.

Higher on the heel, paler than pure cream
Leaner on the sidewalk
Cuttin' through the steam
After claws and feathers
He took skin and bone
Shaped it like an hourglass
And made the angels moan.

Oh! Here's a little heat boys
To straighten out them curls
Now there ain't been no angels round
Since God invented girls.

Now I know what Brian Wilson meant
Every time I step outside
I see what Heaven sent
There may be seven wonders
Created for this world
But one is all we need
Since God invented girls.

Oh, I know what Brian Wilson meant
Every time I step outside
I see what Heaven sent
There may be seven wonders
Created for this world
But one is all we need
Since God invented girls.

sixty years on

Who'll walk me down to church when I'm sixty years of age
When the ragged dog they gave me has been ten years in the grave
And senorita play guitar, play it just for you
My rosary has broken, and my beads have all slipped through.

You've hung up your great coat and you've laid down your gun
You know the war you fought in wasn't too much fun.

And the future you're giving me holds nothing for a gun
I've no wish to be living sixty years on.

Yes I'll sit with you and talk, let your eyes relive again
I know my vintage prayers would be very much the same
And Magdalena plays the organ, plays it just for you
Your choral lamp that burns so low when you are passing through.

And the future you're giving me holds nothing for a gun
I've no wish to be living sixty years on.

skyline pigeon

Turn me loose from your hands
Let me fly to distant lands
Over green fields, trees and mountains
Flowers and forest fountains
Home along the lanes of the skyway

For this dark and lonely room
Projects a shadow cast in gloom
And my eyes are mirrors
Of the world outside
Thinking of the way
That the wind can turn the tide
And these shadows turn
From purple into grey

For just a Skyline Pigeon
Dreaming of the open
Waiting for the day
He can spread his wings
And fly away again
Fly away Skyline Pigeon fly
Towards the dreams
You've left so very far behind

Just let me wake up in the morning
To the smell of new-mown hay
To laugh and cry, to live and die
In the brightness of my day

I want to hear the pealing bells
Of distant churches sing
But most of all please free me
From this aching metal ring
And open out this cage towards the sun

slave

There's a river running sweat right through our land,
Driven by a man with a bullwhip in his hand
And I've taken just as much as I can stand.
Oh, we've got to free our brothers from their shackles if we can.

Most nights I have to watch my woman cry,
Every day I watch the colonel smile,
His painted ladies riding in from town
I swear one day I'm gonna burn that whorehouse to the ground.

Slave! Slave!
To fight the violence we must brave,
Hold on strong
To the love God gave, slave.

There's a rumour of a war that's yet to come
That may free our families and our sons,
It may lay green lands to barren wastes,
The price of release is a bitter blow to face.

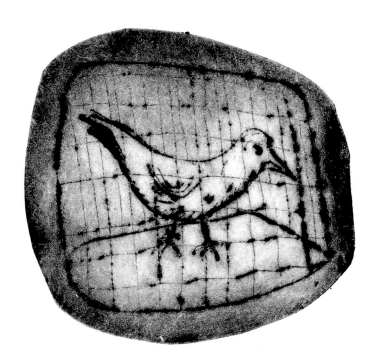

sleeping with the past

Like a thief he's come
Like a thief he's gone
He's stolen your tears one by one
You're proud to love him
It's a foolish sign
You're a broken heart
At the scene of the crime

And the night drags on
Oh and the fever burns
Come to your senses
Everybody learns
Ooh you sleep in sweet fire
Lost and blue
You're an empty doll
In the power of a fool

Don't go sleeping with the past
Don't go praying he'll come back
Take a deep breath and deny
You could love a man like that

Don't go sleeping with the past
Don't go waking with a dream
There's no tenderness that's left
In the cracks you step between

If it looks like rain
If it makes no sounds
It's an echo of pain on common ground
Love's like a junkie
Addiction's a fact
Passion's a monkey
You can't keep off your back

Don't go sleeping with the past
Don't go praying he'll come back
Take a deep breath and deny
You could love a man like that

Don't go sleeping with the past
Don't go waking with a dream
There's no tenderness that's left
In the cracks you step between

But he takes love
And he turns it cold
He's just an iceman honey
Ain't got no heart of gold
But he sees you and he runs from you
Come on and shake this shadow
That you're clinging to
And he'll hurt you
And he'll run from you
Come on and shake this shadow
That you're clinging to

Don't go sleeping with the past
Don't go praying he'll come back
Take a deep breath and deny
You could love a man like that
Don't go sleeping with the past
Don't go waking with a dream
There's no tenderness left
In the cracks you step between

slow down georgie (she's poison)

Hey there Georgie gotta couple of things to say
One you're my friend, and two it's hurting me
Seeing you act this way
But my hands are tied and I can only try
To talk you out of a fall
'Cause the reputation of the woman you dating's
About as nasty as the Berlin wall

Slow down Georgie she's poison
Man you've gotta watch yourself
She's gonna get in your head, she's gonna crawl in your bed
You're just a stepping stone to someone else

Slow down Georgie she's poison
She's just another divorcee
An undercover lover of a hundred
Other little fish in the sea

You better cut her loose before she gets her hooks in you
If you gave her the world, and it was covered in pearls
She'd only ask for the moon
She's got you hypnotised, with her big brown eyes
And a body that could stop a clock
But if you think your face ain't gonna be replaced
Georgie boy you're in for a shock

slow rivers

The weather man he looks confused
Shakes his fist at the sky like you used to do
But you don't remember things like that do you
The balance was uneven but I'm breaking through

Slow rivers run cold
Shallow waters never sank so low
I thought I'd drown and you'd never know
You're a slow river and you run so cold

The winter here don't believe in God
The bitter wind just bites through me like a wild dog
I still see your eyes tonight like headlight through the fog
But one foot in your door oh that's all I ever got

Slow rivers run cold
Shallow waters never sank so low
I thought I'd drown and you'd never know
You're a slow river and you run so cold

Chances are you'll reappear
Swim my way in a flood of tears
No place to hide your conscience so
You're a sinking ship with no place to go

snow queen

You remind me so much
Of her when you're walking
Where everything's perfect
And nobody's talking

You're a cushion uncrumpled
You're a bed that's unruffled
And I believe in the snow queen
That's somewhere in the hills
She's got the world on a string

If I was bone china bone china around
Under your spell like icicles
Upon a frosty cave
The snow queen reigns in a colder land
Behind cold black gates

Your talons are tested
They're polished and shaved
Your talents are wasted
On men with no taste

social disease

My bulldog is barking in the backyard
Enough to raise a dead man from his grave.
And I can't concentrate on what I'm doing,
Disturbance going to crucify my days.

And the days they get longer and longer
And the night-time is a time of little use.
For I just get ugly and older,
I get juiced on Mateus and just hang loose.

And I get bombed for breakfast in the morning,
I get bombed for dinnertime and tea.
I dress in rags, smell a lot, and have a (real good time) (heart of gold),
I'm a genuine example of a social disease.

My landlady lives in a caravan,
Well that is when she isn't in my arms.
And it seems I pay the rent in human kindness,
But my liquor also helps to grease her palm. .

And the ladies are all getting wrinkles,
And they're falling apart at the seams.
While I just get high on tequila,
And see visions of vineyards in my dreams.

solar prestige a gammon

Oh ma cameo molesting
Kee pa a poorer for tee
Solar prestige a gammon
Lantern or turbert paw kwee

Solar prestige a gammon
Kook kar kyrie kay salmon
Hair ring molassis abounding
Common lap kitch sardin a poor floudin

Cod ee say oo pay a loto
My zeta prestige toupay a floored
Ray indee pako a gammon
Solar prestige a pako can nord.

someone saved my life tonight

When I think of those East End lights
Muggy nights,
The curtains drawn in the little room downstairs.
Prima Donna lord you really should have been there,
Sitting like a princess perched in her electric chair.
And it's one more beer,
And I don't hear you anymore.
We've all gone crazy lately,
My friend's out there rolling round the basement floor.

And someone saved my life tonight, sugar bear.
You almost had your hooks in me didn't you dear.
You nearly had me roped and tied,
Altar-bound, hypnotised,
Sweet freedom whispered in my ear
You're a butterfly,
And butterflys are free to fly,
Fly away, high away bye bye.

I never realised the passing hours
Of evening showers,
A slip noose hanging in my darkest dreams.
I'm strangled by your haunted social scene
Just a pawn out-played by a dominating queen.
It's four-o-clock in the morning
Damn it!
Listen to me good.
I'm sleeping with myself tonight
Saved in time, thank God my music's still alive.

And I would have walked head on into the deep end of a river
Clinging to your stocks and bonds
Paying your H.P. demands forever.
They're coming in the morning with a truck to take me home
Someone saved my life tonight, someone saved my life tonight,
Someone saved my life tonight, someone saved my life tonight,
Someone saved my life tonight.
So save your strength and run the field you play alone.

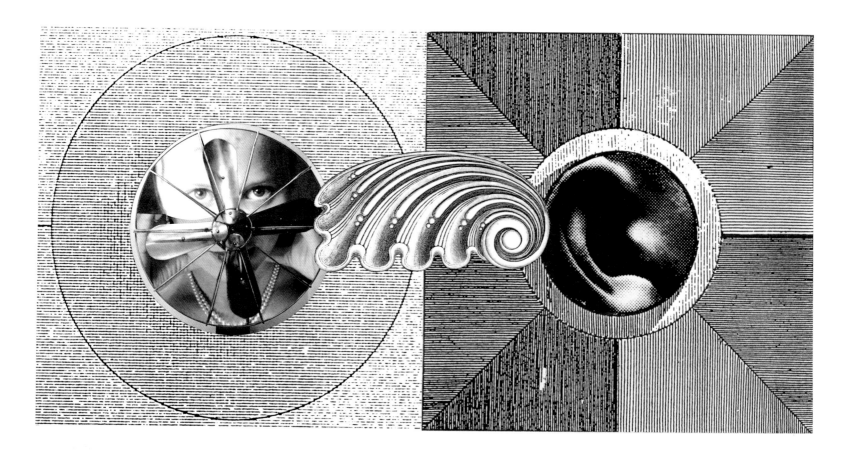

someone's final song

He died when the house was empty,
When the maid had gone.
He put a pen to paper for one final song.
He wrote –
'Oh babe, it's the only way.
I know it's wrong but I can't stand
To go on living, to go on living, living life this way.

And I don't know what the time is,
Or what the next line is.
Or how you're going to take the news.
But if I had my life again.
Ooh ooh
I wouldn't change a thing.
I'd let nobody – I'd let nobody
Stand inside my shoes.

Oh something's gotten hold of me,
This home is not the home it used to be.
I've gathered dust like the dying flowers,
And I've drunk myself sober – oh oh
After hours and hours.'

son of
your father

I'll catch the tramline in the morning
With your leave, Van Bushell said
He had further heard the cock crow
As he stumbled out the shed

Then blind Joseph came towards him
With a shotgun in his arms
He said you'll pay me twenty dollars
Before you leave my farm

Van Bushell saw the hook
Which replaced Joseph's hand
He said now calm you down my brother
Let's discuss this man to man

It's no good you getting angry
We must try to act our age
You're pursuing your convictions
Like some hermit in a cage

You're the son of your father
Try a little bit harder
Do for me as he would do for you
With blood and water, bricks and mortar
He built for you a home
You're the son of your father
So treat me as your own

Well slowly Joseph well he lowered the rifle
And he emptied out the shells
Van Bushell he come towards him
He shook his arm and wished him well

He said now hey blind man that is fine
But I sure can't waste my time
So move aside and let me go my way
I've got a train to ride

Well Joseph turned around
His grin was now a frown
He said let me just refresh your mind
Your manners boy seem hard to find

There's two men lying dead as nails
On an East Virginia farm
For charity's an argument
That only leads to harm

So be careful when they're kind to you
Don't you end up in the dirt
Just remember what I'm saying to you
And you likely won't get hurt

Sorry Seems To Be The Hardest Word

What have I got to do to make you love me
What have I got to do to make you care,
What do I do when lightning strikes me
And I wake to find that you're not there?

What have I got to do to make you want me,
What have I got to do to be heard,
What do I say when it's all over?
And sorry seems to be the hardest word

It's sad (so sad)
It's a sad, sad situation
And it's getting more and more absurd
It's sad, (so sad)
Why can't we talk it over?
Oh it seems to me
that sorry seems to be the hardest word

What have I got to do to make you love me
What have I got to do to be heard,
What do I do when lightning strikes me
What have I got to do?
What have I got to do
When sorry seems to be the hardest word?

138

soul glove

You say today was not so easy
Pressure tends to bet the best of you
Well don't let them break your spirit
Keep the faith and you will come on through

And I'll head home for the weekend
You're tired and you know I'll understand
Just be waiting on the frontsteps baby when I get there
And take a giant step into my hands

And slip into my soul glove
Pull it on we got a tight fit
Never take it off
And baby if the seam's rough
And honey if the skin's soft
You and me we go together
Oh like a soul glove
Look at me don't you believe me
Cheating hangs a noose around your neck
To shave in someone else's mirror
Is one desire I haven't dreamed of yet

But I'll head home for the weekend
You're tired and you know I'll understand
Just be waiting on the frontsteps baby when I get there
And take a giant step into my hands

And slip into my soul glove
Pull it on we got a tight fit
Oh never take it off
And baby if the seam's rough
And honey if the skin's soft
You and me we go together
Oh like a soul glove
Soul glove

We go together
Oh we go together like a soul glove
Pull it on we got a tight fit
We go together
Baby baby baby soul glove soul glove.

spiteful child

I don't want to worry you none, but I got the hurt on the run
I just cut out the poison that was in me so long.
Watching you tear out my heart, only gave me the last laugh
Watching you tear out your hair, is gonna be the best part
Oh I've been shaken down by a spiteful child
I've slapped a worried frown on that evil smile
I've been taken down by a spiteful child
I've turned the tables round and it drives you wild
Oh you spiteful child

You'd better be ready to run, now I've got you under the gun
I put my money on vengeance before this race had begun
Breaking the spirit in me, only added to your conceit
Playing you at your own game, is going to make it complete
Oh I've been shaken down by a spiteful child
Turn the tables round and it drives you wild
Oh you spiteful child

I don't want to worry you none, but I got the hurt on the run
I just cut out the poison that was in me so long
Watching you tear out my heart, only gave me the last laugh
Watching you tear out your hair, is gonna be the best part
Oh I've been shaken down by a spiteful child
I've been taken down by a spiteful child
I've turned the tables round and it drives you wild
Oh you spiteful child
Spiteful spiteful

step into christmas

Welcome to my Christmas song,
I'd like to thank you for the year.
So I'm a-sending you this Christmas card
To say it's nice to have you here.

I'd like to sing about all the things
Your eyes and mine can see,
So hop aboard your turn-table
Oh, step into Christmas with me, yeah.

Step into Christmas, let's join together,
We can watch the snow fall for ever and ever,
Eat, drink and be merry, come along with me,
Step into Christmas, the admission's free.

Take care in all you do next year
And keep smiling through the days.
If we can help to entertain you,
Oh, we will find the ways.

So merry Christmas, one and all,
There's no place I'd rather be
Than asking you if you'll oblige
Stepping into Christmas with me.

Step into Christmas, let's join together,
We can watch the snow fall for ever and ever,
Eat, drink and be merry, come along with me
Step into Christmas, the admission's free.

stinker

Say what you will but I'm a stinker
I come crawling up out of my hole
Dirt in my toes, dirt up my nose
I'm a perfect curse to pest control.

Seeds and weeds and muddy meals
Crawling around the earth
Down in the ground where the sun don't pound
Oh, I hibernate in English turf.

Better believe it I'm a stinker
Burnin' vermin stink
Watch me get as high as a heat wave, honey
Tell me what your hound dogs think.

Set in my styles with a beady eye
I got connections with the underground
Call me a common rodent boy
Sitting here safe and sound.

Some mole hill mother sauntered by
Acting like the ace of spades
Don't give that cutey no reason to shoot me
When I'm living on the eggs she layed.

stone's throw from hurtin'

Help me information,
Get emotion on the line
This war that's ragin' in my heart's getting harder
All the time
Our painted smiles are cracking,
Our worried friends just frown
We gotta runaway train on an empty track
That's trying to run us down

And I'm a stone's throw from hurtin'
Everything we put together
Knee deep in learning about burning this bridge forever
I'm a stone's throw, a stone's throw
A stone's throw from hurtin'
And I know it's never gonna get no better

Crippled conversation hangs inside this house
Our voices just get ugly
When our love gets all talked out
Your goodnight kiss ain't hungry,
Our touches don't connect
We're just a couple of kids with a broken toy
That our idle fingers wrecked

And I'm a stone's throw from hurtin'
Everything we ever put together
Knee deep in learning about burning this bridge forever
I'm a stone's throw, a stone's throw
Stones throw from hurtin'
And I know it's never gonna get no better

Some things get broken
When stones get thrown
Some things get better
When you leave what you love

And let what you love alone
When stones get thrown
Some things bet better
When you leave what you love
And let what you love alone

And I'm a stone's throw from hurtin'
Everything we ever put together
Knee deep in learning about burning this bridge forever
I'm a stone's throw, a stone's throw
Stone's throw from hurtin'
And I know it's never gonna get no better

street kids

They must have had the whole thing planned
There must have been a hundred,
Can we make a stand
I think we'll be outnumbered.
If I'd had the chance
Then I could understand
Why I'm a juvenile delinquent
In an East End gang.

And if you think you've seen gasoline
Swlmmin' in my eyes
Don't be alarmed
Tell yourself
It's good to be – it's good to be alive.

It's just another street kid on your tail
Running on the wrong side of the rails
In my great lace tie and my hand-me-downs,
I run the toughest bunch this side of town
These street kids makin' news just being around.

I've been Bottled and been Brained
Squealers can't be trusted,
If we fight tonight
You can bet we'll all be busted.
I'd like to break away from the rut I'm in
But beggars can't be choosers
I was born to sin.

suit of wolves

Looking back in anger
On this dirty little town
It stained your dress carved up my face
Put a wedge between our state of grace.

Something so young and pretty
Should never be released
We place our bets we take our pick
They wind up in the belly of the beast.

And when you can't get what you want
You take anything you can
So I wear this suit of wolves at night
I slip it on how come it feels so right
I getta hungry man
When I can't get what I want
I take anything I can
I wear a suit of wolves

I wear a suit of wolves

Just across from Friday
The weekend circus rolls
I cross my heart turn on the charm
I say my prayers between two hungry arms.

There's a string of dangerous flowers
All around my bed
There's some want rings and some just want
And those who'd like to see me dead.

And when you can't get what you want
You take anything you can
So I wear this suit of wolves at night
I slip it on how come it feels so right
I getta hungry man
When I can't get what I want
I take anything I can
I wear a suit of wolves.

I wear a suit of wolves.

When you can't get what you want
You take anything you can
So I wear this suit of wolves at night
I slip it on how come it feels so right
I getta hungry man
When I can't get what I want
I take anything I can
I wear a suit of wolves.

I wear a suit of wolves.

susie (dramas)

I got frostbitten in the winter
Ice skating on the river
With my pretty little black-eyed girl.
She'd make your darn toes curl
Just to see her.

I got a fringe front on my buggy,
I got a frisky little colt in a hurry
And a pretty little black-eyed Susie by my side.

Well she sure knows how to use me
Pretty little black-eyed Susie,
Playing hooky with my heart all the time.
Living with her funky family
In a derelict old alley
Down by the river where we share a little lovin' in the moonshine.

I'm an old hayseed harp player,
I'm the hit of the county fair
With my pretty little black-eyed girl,
Living proof as she swirls,
She's a dancer.

sweat it out

No ceiling on hard living
Peace keepers keep on breathing
Can't deny eye for eye
It's open season
She-devils were ruling Britain
Hey girl stick it in your purse
Call it treason

Band aids on dead doorways
No heroes in the Bat Cave
Don't give me Tears for Fears
Give me tears of rage
Fires burn with black smoke
Oil slicks put us on the ropes
Man it's hard to handle
When the bank's broke

Don't kowtow
Don't bow down
Loosen up
Get the lead out
Backs up let 'em shout
Backs up sweat it out
When your back's up
Sweat it out
Backs up
Sweat it out

Hope froze in the cold weather
No ice on a greasy river
Liberty and John Doe
Stand and shiver
War waits when lines form
The baby sitter in a uniform
Knocking down your door
For your rice and corn

No ceiling on hard living
Peace keepers keep on breathing
Can t deny eye for eye
It's open season
Dictate to my reason
She-devils were ruling Britain
Hey girl stick it in your purse
Call it treason

sweet painted lady

I'm back on dry land once again
Opportunity awaits me like a rat in a drain,
We're all hunting honey with money to burn
Just a short time to show you the tricks that we've learned.

If the boys all behave themselves here
Well there's pretty young ladies and beer in the rear,
You won't need a gutter to sleep in tonight
The prices I charge here will see you all right.

She lays down beside me again
My sweet painted lady, the one with no name,
Many have used her and many still do
There's a place in the world for a woman like you.

Oh! Sweet painted lady
Seems it's always been the same,
Getting paid for being laid
Guess that's the name of the game.

Forget us we'll have gone very soon
Just forget we ever slept in your rooms,
And we'll leave the smell of the sea in your beds
Where love's just a job and nothing is said.

JKWadley 94

take me to the pilot

If you feel that it's real
I'm on trial

And I'm here in your prison
Like a coin in your mint
I am dented and spent with high treason.

Through a glass eye, your throne
Is the one danger zone
Take me to the Pilot for control
Take me to the Pilot of your soul
Take me to the Pilot
Lead me to his chamber
Take me to the Pilot
I am but a stranger.

Well I know he's not old and I'm told he's a virgin
For he may be she
But what I'm told is never for certain.

Through a glass eye, your throne
Is the one danger zone
Take me to the Pilot for control
Take me to the Pilot of your soul
Take me to the Pilot
Lead me to his chamber
Take me to the Pilot
I am but a stranger.

talking old soldiers

Why hello, say can I buy you another glass of beer?
Well thanks a lot, that's kind of you,
It's nice to know you care
These days there's so much going on
No one seems to wanna know
I may be just an old soldier to some
But I know how it feels to grow old

Yea that's right
You can see me here most every night
You'll always see me staring
At the walls and at the lights
Funny I remember oh it's years ago I'd say
I'd stand at that bar
With my friends who've passed away
And drink three time the beer that I can drink today
Yes I know how it feels to grow old

I know what they're saying son
There goes old mad Joe again
Well, I maybe mad at that, I've seen enough
To make a man go out his brains
Well do they know what it's like
To have a graveyard as a friend
'Cause that's where they are boy, all of them
Don't seem likely I'll get friends like that again

Well it's time I moved off,
But it's been great just listening to you
And I might even see yer next time I'm passing through
You're right there's so much going on
No one seems to wanna know
So keep well, keep well old friend
And have another drink on me
Just ignore all the others, you've got your memories.

teacher I need you

I was sitting in the classroom,
Trying to look intelligent,
In case the teacher looked at me,
She was long and she was lean,
She's a middle-aged dream,
And that lady means the whole world to me.

It's a natural achievement,
Conquering my homework,
With her image, pounding in my brain,
She's an inspiration,
For my graduation,
And she helps to keep the classroom sane.

Oh, teacher I need you,
Like a little child,
You got something in you,
To drive a schoolboy wild.

You give me education,
In the lovesick blues,
Help me get straight, come out and say,
Teacher I, Teacher I, Teacher I,
Teacher I need you.

I have to write a letter,
Tell about my feelings,
Just to let her know the scene,
Focus my attention,
On some further education,
In connection with the birdies and the bees.

So I'm sitting in the classroom,
I'm looking like a zombie,
I'm waiting for the bell to ring,
I've got John Wayne stances,
I've got Erroll Flynn advances,
And it doesn't mean a doggone thing.

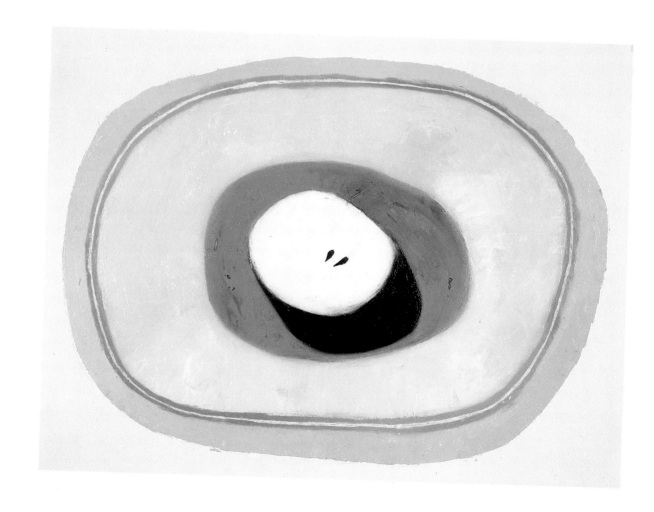

tell me what the papers say

I spy headlines, newsprint tells lies
Tell me what the papers say

Save lives don't drive, everybody's got to die someday
At least that's what the papers say

Coal mines, closed down
Nobody's working underground today

More jails, peace for sale
Japanese still killing whales

Teen dreams
On two inch screens
Lipstick boys all look like queens
Least that's what the papers say

I spy headlines, newsprint tells lies
Tell me what the papers say

Save lives don't drive, everybody's got to die someday
At least that's what the papers say

Dope and pills, guns kill
Death just buys cheap thrills

Coal mines, closed down
Nobody's working underground today

Teen dreams
On two inch screens
Lipstick boys all look like queens
Least that's what the papers say
Tell me what the papers say
Tell me what the papers say

Coal mines, closed down
Nobody's working underground today

Dope and pills, guns kill
Death just buys cheap thrills

Teen dreams, on two inch screens
Lipstick boys all look like queens

tell me when the whistle blows

There's a dusty old gutter he's lying in now,
He's blind and he's old
And there's a bottle that rolls down the road.
Me I'm young and I'm so wild,
And I still feel the need for your apron strings once in awhile.
For there's taxi cabs hootin'
And I can't be foot loose forever.
My suitcase it's a cheap one
My darlin' she's a dear one,
My head's feelin' light as a feather.

Take my ears and tell me when the whistle blows.
Wake me up and tell me when the whistle blows.
Long lost and lonely boy
You're just a black sheep going home.
I want to feel your wheels of steel
Underneath my itchin' heels.
Take my money
Tell me when the whistle blows.
Part of me asked the young man for the time,
With a cold vacant stare of undue concern
He said 'Nine.'
It's not so bad but I really do love the land,
And rather all this than those diamanté lovers
In Hyde Park holding hands.
Blowing heat through my fingers
Trying to kill off this cold.
Will the street kids remember
Can I still shoot a fast cue,
Has this country kid still got his soul.

texan love song

I heard from a friend you'd been messin' around,
With a cute little thing I'd been dating uptown,
Well I don't know if I like that idea much,
Well you'd better stay clear I might start acting rough.

You out of town guys sure think you're real keen,
Think all of us boys here are homespun and green,
But that's wrong my friend so get this through your head,
We're tough and we're Texan with necks good and red.

So it's Ki-i-yippie-yi-yi,
You long hairs are sure gonna die,
Our American home was clean till you came,
And kids still respected the president's name.

And the eagle still flew in the sky,
Hearts filled with national pride,
Then you came along with your drug-crazy songs,
Goddamit you're all gonna die.

How dare you sit there and drink all our beer,
Oh it's made for us workers who sweat, spit and swear,
The minds of our daughters are poisoned by you,
With your communistic politics and them negro blues.

Well I'm gonna quit talking and take action now,
Run all of you fairies clean out of this town,
Oh I'm dog tired of watchin' you mess up our lives,
Spending the summertime naturally high.

the ballad of danny bailey
(1909-34)

Some punk with a shotgun
Killed young Danny Bailey
In cold blood, in the lobby
Of a downtown motel.

Killed him in anger,
A force he couldn't handle,
Helped pull the trigger
That cut short his life
And there's not many knew him
The way that we did,
Sure enough he was a wild one
But then aren't most hungry kids?

Now it's all over Danny Bailey,
And the harvest is in.
Dillinger's dead
I guess the cops won again.
Now it's all over Danny Bailey,
And the harvest is in.

We're running short of heroes
Back up here in the hills,
Without Danny Bailey
We're gonna have to break up our stills.

So make his grave well
'Cause Kentucky loved him.
Born and raised proper
I guess life just bugged him.

And he found faith in danger,
A life style he lived by,
A runnin' gun youngster
In a sad restless age.

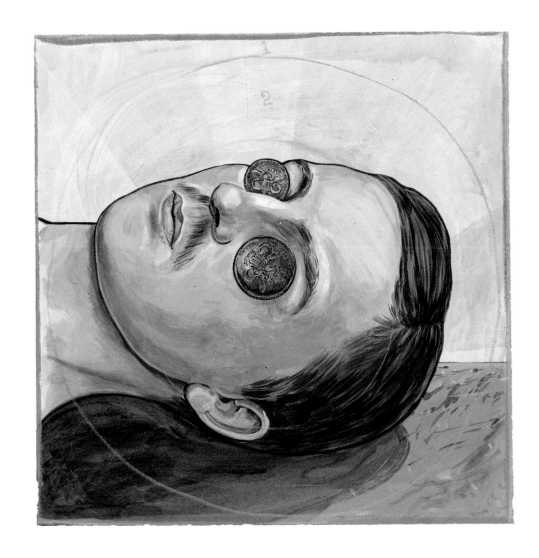

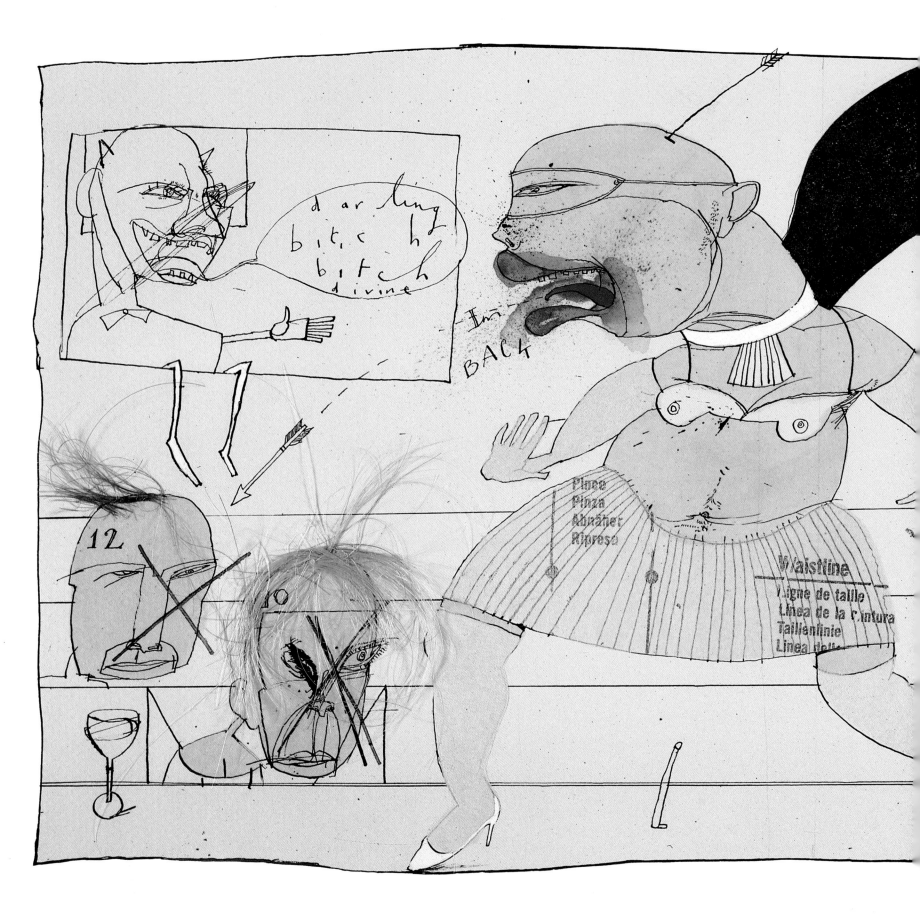

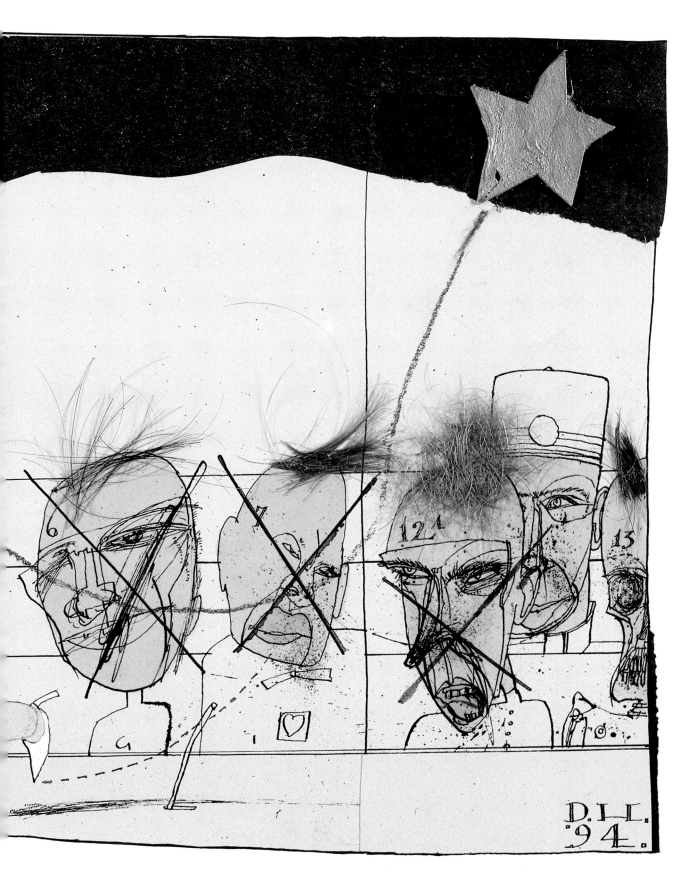

the bitch is back

I was justified when I was five
Raisin' cane
I spit in your eye
Times are changin'
Now the poor get fat
But the fever's gonna catch you
When the bitch gets back,
Oh, Oh, Oh.

Eat meat on Friday
That's all right
Even like steak
On a Saturday night
I can bitch the best
At your social do's
I get high in the evening
Sniffing pots of glue,
Oh, Oh, Oh.

I'm a bitch I'm a bitch
Oh, the bitch is back
Stone cold sober as a matter of fact
I can bitch, I can bitch
'Cause I'm better than you
It's the way that I move
The things that I do.

I entertain by picking brains
Sell my soul
By dropping names.
I don't like those!
My God, what's that!
Oh, it's full of nasty habits
When the bitch gets back.

the cage

Have you ever lived in a cage
Where you live to be whipped and be tamed
For I've never loved in a cage
Or talked to a friend or just waved.

Well I walk while they talk about virtue
Just raised on my backlegs and snarled
Watched you kiss your old daddy with passion
And tell dirty jokes as he died.

But I'm damned when I really care there
For the cellar's the room in your lives
Where you lace yourself with bad whisky
And close the cage doors on your life.

Well I pray while you bathe in bad water
Sing songs that I learnt as a boy
Then break all the bones in my body
On the bars you can never destroy.

Have you ever lived in a cage
Where you live to be whipped and be tamed
For I've never loved in a cage
Or talked to a friend or just waved.

the camera never lies

Hey girl. I see you tempt the night
I see you take a bite
You can tell me you were home
But the camera never lies.

You walk out in disguise
To pull the wool over my eyes
You play me for a fool
To believe your alibis.

And you can count on being safe as houses
Underestimate my eyes
But you can't argue with the image
The camera never lies.
There's no distance put between us
Safe enough for you to hide
I'm watching all of your secrets
The camera never lies.

I recommend first prize
For acting so surprised
For acting like you love me
The camera never lies.

I'll take my wounded pride
I'll take it on the chin
Your profile fills the frame
How good you look on film.

And you can count on being safe as houses
Underestimate my eyes
But you can't argue with the image
The camera never lies.
There's no distance put between us
Safe enough for you to hide
I'm watching all of your secrets
The camera never lies.

Smoke screens and sweet deceiving
Replace the face of trust
The shutter falls each time you meet him
A negative becomes my plus.

And you can count on being safe as houses
Underestimate my eyes
But you can't argue with the image
The camera never lies.
There's no distance put between us
Safe enough for you to hide
I am watching all of your secrets
The camera never lies.

the fox

Being wirey and thinking loudly
About the things sent to make you move
You can't help it, there's no one in this world
Knows you just, just they way you do
So we keep darting through the holes
As the hunter and the fox
Run the gauntlet's savage road

Winter's heavy and partly cloudy
And the snowfall leaves the tracks that catch a few
If you're wiley, you will leave them lying
Snared up in the traps that they set for you
And it's an evergreen affair
As temptation taunts the fox
Into the hunter's waiting lair

And for mile after mile you'll never see me tire
You'll never see me slow down, for a while
'Cause I am the fox, like it or not
I'm always gonna be there running over the rock
Yes I am the fox, a fascinating cross
As sharp as a whip and tough as an ox
Yes I am the fox

It may sound crazy but it's often lonely
And the restless heart should be captured once in a while
Then you can use them, and you often fool them
Into believing whatever you desire
So I'll keep moving through the night
The hunter and the hunted
On their designated flights

the greatest discovery

Peering out of tiny eyes
The grubby hands that gripped the rail
Wiped the window clean of frost
As the morning air laid on the latch
A whistle awakened someone there
Next door to the nursery just down the hall
A strange new sound you never heard before
A strange new sound that makes boys explore
Tread neat so small those little feet
Amid the morning his small heart beats
So much excitement yesterday
That must be rewarded, must be displayed.

Large hands lift him through the air
Excited eyes contain him there
The eyes of those he loves and knows
But what's this extra bed just here
His puzzled head tipped to one side
Amazement swims in those bright green eyes
Glancing down upon this thing
That makes strange sounds, strange sounds that sing
In those silent happy seconds
That surround the sound of this event
A parent smile is made in moments
They have made for you a friend
And all you ever learned from them
Until you grew much older
Did not compare with when they said
This is your brand new brother.

the king must die

No man's a jester playing Shakespeare
Round your throne room floor
While the juggler's act is danced upon
The crown that you once wore.

And sooner or later,
Everybody's kingdom must end,
And I'm so afraid your courtiers,
Cannot be called best friends.

Caesar's had your troubles
Widows had to cry
While mercenaries in cloisters sing
And the King must die.

Some men are better staying sailors
Take my word and go
But tell the ostler that his name was
The very first they chose.

And if my hands are stained forever
And the altar should refuse me
Would you let me in, would let me in,
Should I cry sanctuary.

Caesar's had your troubles
Widows had to cry
While mercenaries in cloisters sing
And the King must die.

No man's a jester playing Shakespeare
Round your throne room floor
While the juggler's act is danced upon
The crown that you once wore.

The King is dead
The King is dead
The King is dead
Long Live the King.

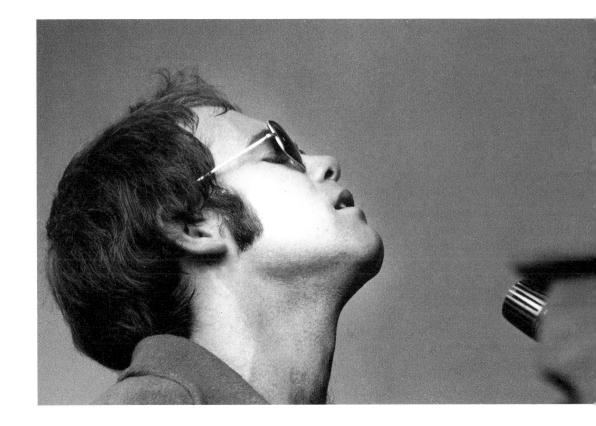

the last song

Yesterday you came to lift me up
As light as straw and brittle as a bird
Today I weigh less than a shadow on the wall
Just one more whisper of a voice unheard

Tomorrow leave the windows open
As fear grows please hold me in your arms
Won't you help me if you can to shake this anger
I need your gentle hands to keep me calm

'Cause I never thought I'd lose
I only thought I'd win
I never dreamed I'd feel
This fire beneath my skin
I can't believe you love me
I never thought you'd come
I guess I misjudged love
Between a father and his son

Things we never said come together
The hidden truth no longer haunting me
Tonight we touched on the things that were never spoken
That kind of understanding sets me free.

the north

Have you seen the North
That cold grey place
Don't want its shadow anymore
On my face
A man grows bitter
We're a bitter race
Some of us never get to see
A better place

In the Northern Skies
There was a steel cloud
It used to follow me around
But I don't see it now
There's a farm in the rain
And a little farmhouse
There were a young man's eyes
Looking south

The North was my mother
But I no longer need her
You trade your roots and your dust
For a face in the river

And a driven rain that washes you
To a different shore
There's a North in us all
But my North can't hold me any more

The North was my mother
But I no longer need her
You trade your roots and your dust
For a face in the river
And a driven rain that washes you
To a different shore
There's a North in us all
But my North can't hold me anymore.

The driven rain that washes you
To a different shore
There's a North in us all
But my North can't hold me anymore.

the one

I saw you dancing out the ocean
Running fast along the sand
A spirit born of earth and water
Fire flying from your hands

In the instant that you love someone
In the second that the hammer hits
Reality runs up your spine
And the pieces finally fit

And all I ever needed was the One
Like freedom feels where wild horses run
When stars collide like you and I
No shadows block the sun
You're all I've ever needed
Baby you're the one

There are caravans we follow
Drunken nights in dark hotels
When chances breathe between the silence
Where sex and love no longer gel

For each man in his time is Cain
Until he walks along the beach
And see his future in the water
A long lost heart within his reach

And all I ever needed was the One
Like freedom feels where wild horses run
When stars collide like you and I
No shadows block the sun
Oh you're all I've ever needed
Ooh baby you're the one.

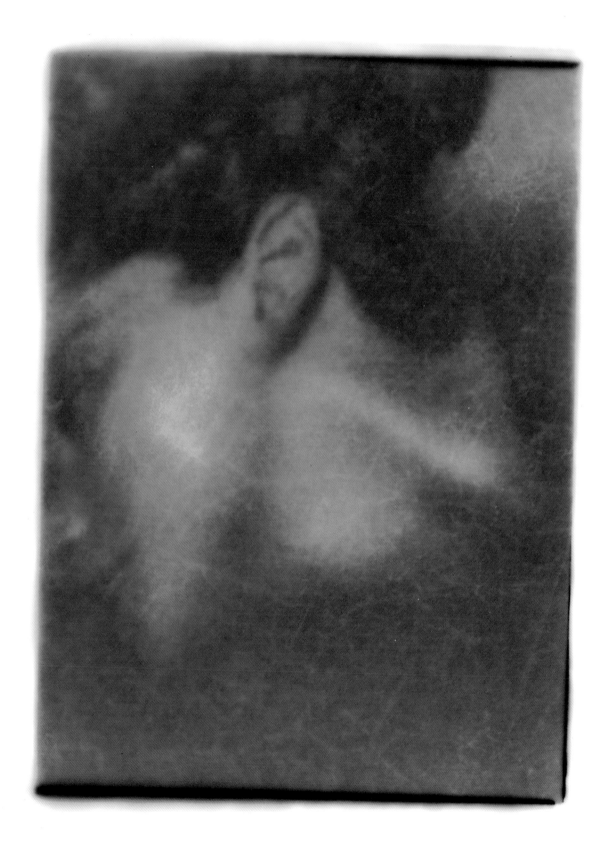

the retreat

They laid beneath the pine trees
With their caps over their eyes
They were drunk with home and mama
As they brushed away the flies
In an instant before the sunrise
They had gunned the rebels down
As their flags were torn at half mast
In the ruins of the town

There were white sails on the water
For the crippled on the beach
There was a lack of ammunition
So the cause was incomplete
When the bugle blew at breakfast
And they knew their ships were in
Sighs of grand assurance were carried on the wind

Take it home, take it low, take responsibilities
Came the message from the front
For the captains, captains' quarters must retreat
Pack the compass, pack the tanks, take the bombs

They just chalked it down in history
But they kept their uniforms
They put their medals on the sideboards
And they went back to their farms
For it was just a mere reminder

That they stood beside their base
That God had saved the chosen few
And the devil took the rest

Take it home, take it low, take responsibilities
Came the message from the front
For the captains, captains' quarters must retreat
Pack the compass, pack the tanks, take the bombs

On the planes above the rock face
Where the sculptured eagles swoop
There's a haunted yell for action
Among the spectres of his troops
It was silent on the coast line
As the crazy angels danced
With the sound of retreating footfall
From his military camp

Take it home, take it low, take responsibilities
Came the message from the front
For the captains, captains' quarters must retreat
Pack the compass, pack the tanks, take the bombs

the scaffold

In Orient where wise I was
To please the way I live
Come give the beggar chance at hand
His life is on his lip

Three score a thousand times
Where once in Amazon
Where Eldorado holds the key
No keeper holds my hand

Unchain the gate of solitude
The ruler says you run
Run hard unto the scaffold high
It's your chance to jump the gun

Oh how high the scaffold grows
The plant life of your widow
In black-lace curtains brought you near
From out the plate glass window

The Minotaur with bloody hands
Is enraged by the sun,
Caged he by the corpses
Brought forth by the dawn

In Orient is as I told
The buckshee hangman swears
For open crypts to silence
Nylon knots to sway by prayer

In Orient where wise I was
To please the way I live
Come give the beggar chance at hand
His life is on his lip

the wide-eyed and laughing

Are you still in control of the boat that you row,
Or do you still cling to me, when it's sinking?
I never condemned you, I only consoled you
When candlelight made me a king.

For the wide-eyed and laughing
Passed like a season
Erasing a passion to sin,
For no one knew better than the tea leaves and the tarots
That the wide-eyed and laughing
Were just one step ahead of the wind.

And the hearts that you played on the porch swing for me
Was a song that I'd heard in the past,
For I had an audience somewhere inside you
That applauded whenever you laughed.

Gone is a word that I now rarely use
Though sometime in the course of the day
I go racing back like a man possessed
By the wide-eyed and laughing daughters of some different age.

this song has no title

Tune me into the wild side of life,
I'm an innocent young child sharp as a knife,
Take me to the garretts where the artists have died,
Show me the court rooms where the judges have lied.

Let me drink deeply from the water and the wine,
Light coloured candles in dark dreary mines,
Look in the mirror and stare at myself
And wonder if that's really me on the shelf.

And each day I learn just a little bit more
I don't know why but I do know what for
If we're all going somewhere let's get there soon,
This song's got no title just words and a tune.

Take me down alleys where the murders are done,
In a vast high-powered rocket to the core of the sun,
Want to read books in the studies of men,
Born on the breeze and die on the wind.

If I was an artist who paints with his eyes,
I'd study my subject and silently cry
Cry for the darkness to come down on me,
For confusion to carry on turning the wheel.

this town

It's closing time the boys are all together at the bar
Staring in their glasses
Looks like another lay off at the yard

Yesterday I heard the union hall come down
They hit it with a wrecking ball
And they try but nothing changes in this town

Cap in hand stood in line
Your family ties are the chains that bind
The endless wheel goes round and round
Chances are you'll never leave this town
Oh oh no

Like a river now the empty streets are flooded out with rain
It's falling on the playground
While the kids get wet playing the same old games

Locked away so many things remind them of war
They tap the pavement with their canes
The good old days ain't so good no more

Cap in hand stood in line
Your family ties are the chains that bind
The endless wheel goes round and round
Chances are you'll never leave this town
Oh oh no

ticking

'An extremely quiet child' they called you in your school report
'He's always taken interest in the subjects that he's taught'
So what was it that brought the squad car screaming up your drive
To notify your parents of the manner in which you died.

At St. Patrick's every Sunday Father Fletcher heard your sins
'Oh, he's unconcerned with competition he never cares to win'
But blood stained a young hand that never held a gun
And his parents never thought of him as their troubled son.

'No you'll never go to Heaven' Mama said
Remember Mama said
Ticking, ticking
'Grow up straight and true blue, run along to bed'
Hear it, hear it, ticking, ticking.

They had you holed up in a downtown bar screaming for a priest
Some gook said 'His brains just snapped' then someone called the police
You'd knifed a negro waiter who had tried to calm you down
Oh, you'd pulled a gun and told them all to lay still on the ground.

Promising to hurt no one, providing they were still
A young man tried to make a break, with tear-filled eyes you killed
That gun butt felt so smooth and warm cradled in your palm
Oh, your childhood cried out in your head, 'They mean to do you harm'.

'Don't ever ride on the devil's knee' Mama said
Remember Mama said
Ticking, ticking
'Pay your penance well, my child, fear where angels tread'
Hear it, hear it, ticking, ticking.

Within an hour the news had reached the media machine
A male Caucasian with a gun had gone berserk in Queens'
The area had been sealed off, the kids sent home from school
Fourteen people lying dead in a bar they called the Kicking Mule.

Oh, they pleaded to your sanity for the sake of those inside
'Throw out your gun, walk out slow just keep your hands held high'
But they pumped you full of rifle shells as you stepped out the door
Oh, you danced in death like a marionette on the vengeance of the law.

'You've slept too long in silence' Mama said
Remember Mama said
Ticking, ticking
'Crazy boy, you'll only wind up, with strange notions in your head'
Hear it, hear it, ticking, ticking.

tiny dancer

Blue jean baby,
L.A. lady, seamstress for the band.
Pretty eyed, pirate smile, you'll marry a music man.
Ballerina. You must have seen her, dancing in the sand.
And now she's in me, always with me,
Tiny Dancer in my hand.

Jesus freaks
Out in the street
Handing tickets out for God.
Turning back she just laughs.
The boulevard is not that bad.

Piano man
He makes his stand
In the auditorium.
Looking on
She sings the songs
The words she knows
The tune she hums.

But oh
How it feels so real lying here
With no one near
Only you, and you can hear me,
When I say softly, slowly.

Hold me closer Tiny Dancer,
Count the headlights
On the highway.
Lay me down in sheets of linen,
You had a busy day today.

tonight

Tonight,
Do we have to fight again
Tonight?
I just want to go to sleep
Turn out the light
But you want to carry grudges
Oh nine times out of ten
I see the storm approaching
Long before the rain starts falling.

Tonight,
Does it have to be the old thing
Tonight?
Oh, it's late, too late
To chase the rainbow that you're after.
I'd like to find a compromise
And place it in your hands
My eyes are blind, my ears can't hear
Oh and I cannot find the time.

Tonight,
Just let the curtains close in silence
Tonight
Why not approach with less defiance
The man who'd love to see you smile,
Who'd love to see you smile
Tonight.

too young

Your mother's eyes look straight through me
Whenever we meet
Your father swears, it'll never be
As long as he breathes

And how many times have they told you
That you're too young
How, how I've ached to hold you
But you're too young

If we don't buy what's right or wrong
Then we are sinners
We were never two to tag along
But we were always winners

And how many people, have told you
that you're too young
And how many jealous hands would love to hold you
'Cause you're too young

Well you're too young to love me
And I'm too old for you
At least that's what they tell us
It's in their book of rules
That you're too young, too young baby you're too young

We could try it for awhile
But they'd get us in the long run
They say that you're too young, baby you're too young

Baby your mother's eyes, look straight through me
Whenever we meet
Oh oh oh whenever we meet
Your father swears, it'll never be, never be
As long as he breathes

And how many times
Oh have I told you
That you're too young
How, how I've ached to hold you
But you're too young

Well you're too young to love me
And I'm too old for you
At least that's what they tell us
You know it's in their book of rules

That you're too young, too young baby you're too young
Oh we could try for awhile
But they'd get us in the end
They'd say that you're too young

Baby you're too young
They'd get us in the end. . .
They'd say that you're too young
Baby you're too young

too low for zero

Six o'clock alarm
I get the wake up call
Let that sucker jingle-jangle,
Ring right off the wall
I'm too low for zero,
I'm too tired to work
Tried one on with a friend last night
And wound up losing my shirt

I'm too low for zero,
I'm on a losing streak
I've got myself in a bad patch lately
I can't seem to get much sleep
I'm too low for zero,
I wind up counting sheep
Nothing seems to make much sense
It's all just Greek to me

You know I'm too low,
Too low, too low for zero

Cuttin' out cups of coffee
Switchin' off the late night news
Puttin' the cat out two hours early,
It isn't any use
I'm too low for zero,
Insomnia attacks
Watching flies with my eyes
Till sunrise
It's daylight when I hit the sack

tortured

I'd like to make this song so simple
Not one I hide my feelings under
Drawn up words of shades of many colours
How can I make them think I'm clever

When I'm really saying that I miss you
It's just a stalemate that I'm going through
No one would ever think that I'm weakening
Although you know I'm always dreaming
Someday you'll be coming home to me

Tortured I've been so tortured by you so many times
And you always love the ones that hurt you
Well I guess those are the times we're blind
Tortured by you

If I'd taken parting easy
It might have been a better lesson
For all concerned who walk through love and hate
How can you swear through your words and music
How to crave and how to move it

It's just a beach you washed my body onto
Then when you know that I am crying
Although your friends can see I'm dying
Slowly from the knife you left in me

Tortured I've been so tortured by you so many times
And you always love the ones that hurt you
Well I guess those are the times we're blind
Tortured by you

It's just a beach you washed my body onto
Nobody will know that I've been crying
Although your friends could see I'm dying
Slowly from the knife you left in me

Tortured I've been so tortured by you so many times
And you always love the ones that hurt you
Well I guess those are the times we're blind
Tortured by you

They'd say that you're too young

Baby you're too young
They'd get us in the end. . .
They'd say that you're too young
Baby you're too young

tower of babel

town of plenty

Snow.
Cement,
And ivory young towers,
Someone called us Babylon
Those hungry hunters
Tracking down the hours.
But where were all your shoulders when we cried,
Were the darlings on the sideline
Dreaming up such cherished lies,
To whisper in your ear before you die.

It's party time for the guys in the tower of Babel.
Sodom meet Gomorrah,
Cain meet Abel.
Have a ball ya'all
See the letches crawl
With the call girls under the table.
Watch 'em dig their graves,
'Cause Jesus don't save the guys
In the tower of Babel.

Junk.
Angel,
This closet's always stacked.
The dealers in the basement
Filling your prescription,
For a brand new heart attack.

But where were all your shoulders when we cried,
Were the doctors in attendance
Saying how they felt so sick inside.
Or was it just the scalpel blade that lied.

I'll say it again
This is not my city
I don't belong
Looking for a town of plenty.
There weren't these thieves
We had something in common
Goals to achieve
We had something in common
Woh oh oh
In a town of plenty.

Ooh can't you see it
This is not my writing
I only asked
If this was a town of plenty
There were many archives
We had no media
Only art survived there
Yeah we had no media
Woh oh oh
In a town of plenty.

And laid across the airstrip
Were the passports and the luggage
All that once remained
Of the rugged individual
And laid across the airstrip
Were the passports and the luggage
Woh oh oh came looking for a town of plenty.

I'll say it again
This is not my city
I only asked
If this was a town of plenty
There were many archives
We had no media
Only art survived there
Yeah we had no media
Woh oh oh
In a town of plenty.

two rooms at the
end of the world

Through a mutual agreement, we got that aching feeling
To look up one another one more time
Tracking down the zip codes
Sealing down those envelopes
Lack of communication on the telephone line.

But don't judge us by distance
Or the difference between us
Try to look at it with an open mind
For where there is one room, you'll always find another
Two rooms, at the end of the world.

Well we've both ridden the wagon bit the tail off the dragon
Borne our swords like steel knights on the highway
Washing down the dirt roads
Hosing off our dirty clothes
Coming to terms with the times that we couldn't but we tried.

Where there is one room, you'll always find another
Two rooms, at the end of the world.
Where there is one room, you'll always find another
Two rooms, at the end of the world.

Door to door they would whisper, will they ever get together
Their rooms are different temperatures I'm told
There's a change in their thinking
And their habits seem uneven
But together the two of them were mining gold.

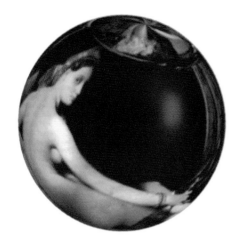

understanding women

Rolling over trying to sleep
And understanding women
Thinking of you out there somewhere
Looking for a new beginning

Just let me be the final word
In the book we haven't written
I won't be another page
In understanding women

I could drive to Mexico
On understanding women
Throw myself against the waves
And answer up to heaven

How come her heart's so stubborn
What's so wrong with giving
Ask the big sky talking
About understanding women

And I'm not just anyone who ever stood outside your door
And I'm not any man you've ever known before
Don't judge this picture by the frame
Every man is not the same
Some men reach beyond the pain of understanding women

Just let me be the final word
In the book we haven't written
I won't be another page
In understanding women

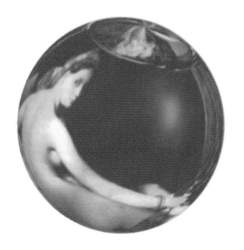

valhalla

The seadogs have all sailed their ships
Into the docks of dawn
While the sirens sit
And comb their hair
And twiddle with their thumbs

Oh Thor, above the mountain
Look down upon your children
This is their heaven
Where they're told
To bring their galleons

Seek you find your place with me
Men of iron, men of steel
Only the brave hear the hammers ring
In the courts of the queens
In the halls of the kings

You can come to Valhala
In your own time
Come to Valhala
Seek and you will find
Valhala

There's long boats in the harbour
Which arrive there every hour
With the souls of the heroes
Whose blood lies on the flowers

And this heaven is the home
Of every man who loves his sword
And he uses it for freedom
To preach the word of Thor

we all fall in love sometimes

Wise men say
It looks like rain today.
It crackled on the speakers
And trickled down the sleepy subway trains.
For heavy eyes could hardly hold us,
Aching legs that often told us
It's all worth it
We all fall in love sometimes.

The full moon's bright
And starlight filled the evening.
We wrote it and I played it,
Something happened it's so strange this feeling.
Naive notions that were childish
Simple tunes that tried to hide it,
But when it comes
We all fall in love sometimes.

I'm not sure 'cause sometimes we're so blind.
Struggling through the day
When even your best friend says,
Don't you find
We all fall in love sometimes.

And only passing time
Could kill the boredom we acquired
Running with the losers for awhile.
But our Empty Sky was filled with laughter
Just before the flood,
Painting worried faces with a smile.

It's hard to feel what's in your hand
Where the gas lamps grow
And the garbage blows
Around the paper stands

And a baby cried
And I saw a light
And I wondered why
There'd be a loss of life
Down here tonight

Western Ford

Down on Western Ford Gateway
That's a place where the dead say
That a man lives no more
That his fair share of days
Down on Western Ford Gateway

Gateway

It flowed upon the cobbled floor
For the bottles dead
And they're drunk again
By the tavern door.

when a woman doesn't want you

She may be lost
She may be out of bounds
All her tenderness and charms
Could be something
A man like me has never found
But in her woman's way
She's still a little girl
The things that she wants
The things that she needs
Oh well, the choice is hers

'Cause you can't take a woman
When she doesn't want you
And you can't be a man
If you're blind to reason
Man might be strong
But true love is stronger
You gotta play it straight
When a woman doesn't want you

Her voice invites
Her eyes say more than words
But her needs and complications
Can tear away
The memory of last night's girl
And if you're weak
Yeah we're all weak sometime
The best things can wait
The best things they come
Oh, when strength is kind

And if you can't read her
Leave her alone
If you don't know by now
She's not someone's prize
And you can't take her home

'Cause you can't take a woman
When she doesn't want you
And you can't be a man
If you'r.e blind to reason
Man might be strong
But true love is stronger
You gotta play it straight
You gotta play it straight
You gotta play it straight
When a woman doesn't want you

whenever you're ready (we'll go steady again)

I lived in a tenement six floors above,
I lent you my records and I lent you my love,
But you left me on the weekend without a by-your-leave,
That's a dirty and a low-down trick, my folks all think you're mean.

But I don't mind, that's kind of nifty,
You always see those break-ups in the movies;
And just like a light you put me out,
Now I'm gonna do my best
To get you back in the nest you came from.

You can tease me if you want to,
Turn your sights on other men,
But whenever you're ready,
Honey, we'll go steady again.

It's nasty without you in my little room,
I miss you like crazy, please come back soon;
I was joking with those things I said,
I couldn't have been thinking,
If you don't come back I think I'll crack,
Just like my old ceiling.

where have all the good times gone?

See the changes here on every street
As time goes marching to a different beat
Moving on into the restless ages
As the kids today find their feet
Young enough to chase our dreams
We were captured by romantic things
Touched by love until it made us cry
How our hearts could fly without wings
Oh won't somebody tell me?

Tell me where have all the good times gone
Say that you remember
Remember all those good old Four Tops songs
Won't somebody tell me
Where have all the good times gone

Stolen moments in the smoky room
Monday mornings that would come too soon
Crazy summers that would never end
When the time was spent lovin' you
Some things never seem to last
Ain't it funny how we missed the past
Love has changed but the clock still turns
While the flame still burns for you
Oh won't somebody tell me?

Tell me where have all the good times gone
Say that you remember
Remember all those good old Four Tops songs
Won't somebody tell me
Where have all the good times gone

They've gone away, gone, They've gone away

It's hard enough to lose the game
And sad to see it played again
What makes you happy for awhile
Is gonna make you smile through the rain
Oh won't somebody tell me
Where have all the good times gone

where's the shoorah?

She grows, she's grown like pampas
Tall in the wind
She's sinful and spiteful,
She's all girl, woman and mother.
She's had my children,
And she's been my lover.

No no no no no no she don't like to fight it,
Once you've been bitten
You get excited.
My mama she really likes her,
She comes for coffee,
And my Mama asked me

So where's the Shoorah, she sang,
You know I hear it again my friend,
Where's the Shoorah, she came upon it,
Waiting to sing her back
'Cause she likes to sing about.
Where's the Shoorah, she sang.
Over and over and over,
Where's the Shoorah, she sang.

where to now st. peter?

I took myself a blue canoe
And I floated like a leaf
Dazzling, dancing,
Half enchanted
In my Merlin sleep

Crazy was the feeling
Restless were my eyes
Insane they took the paddles
My arms they paralysed

So, where to now St. Peter
If it's true I'm in your hands
I may not be a Christian
But I've done all one man can
I understand I'm on the road
Where all that was is gone
So where to now St. Peter
Show me which road I'm on
Which road I'm on

It took a sweet young foreign gun
This lazy life is short
Something for nothing always ending
With a bad report

Dirty was the daybreak
Sudden was the change
In such a silent place as this
Beyond the rifle range.

whipping boy

Ooh yer cruel, ooh yer do
Ooh yer do yer do me wrong
Ooh yer hurt me, ooh yer flirt with
Any old face that comes along

But I won't be your whipping boy
No I won't be your whipping boy
Break me like a little toy
Run me till my feet are sore
But I won't be your whipping boy

Ooh you're wild, ooh you're sly
What you done to me
I was thirty, I look like fifty
Ooh but I feel like sixty-three

It's the illegal kind of lovin'
That keeps my motor runnin'
From the start to the finish line
It's a trashy kind of me
That like to believe
That I'm still tryin'
I'm still tryin'
I'm still tryin', yes I'm tryin'

Ooh you're dirty,
But you're worth it
Ooh but you're way
You're way too young
I could do time if they found out
Look out, San Quentin here I come

whispers

Look at me twice with wildcat eyes
Promise me everything
Except a blue night
Shudder like ice in cut crystal glass
Melt in embraces
Of crazy-eyed past
And whisper, whisper, whispering whispers

Tantamount to a lie with lingering breath
Walking fingers run
Hungry scratches left
Dull chimes ringing like an empty voice
A distant smile framed
Her lips are soft and moist
With whisper, whisper, whispering whispers

And whisper in rhythm your lies
Keep comfort for others
Hurt me with the night
Whisper like cold winds
Close to the bone
Save heaven for lovers
Leave me alone
With your whisper, whisper, whispering whispers

Whisper, whisper, whispering whispers

And whisper in rhythm your lies
Keep comfort for others
Hurt me with the night
Whisper like cold winds
Close to the bone
Save heaven for lovers
Leave me alone
With your whisper, whisper, whispering whisperin'

Whisper in rhythm your lies
Keep comfort for others
Hurt me with the night
Whisper like cold winds
Close to the bone
Save heaven for lovers
Leave me alone
With your whisper, whisper, whispering whispers

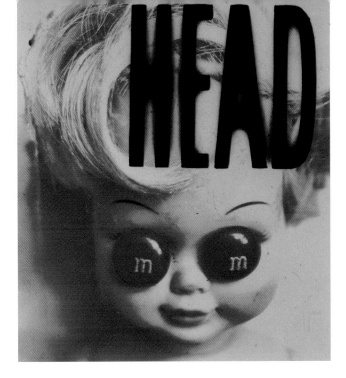

white lady white powder

Dust settles on a thin cloud
Sends a fog drifting to a worn-out crowd
I've had my face to the mirror for twenty-four hours
Staring at a line of white powder

High-priced madness pays the tab
I've scraped too much of nothing from your plastic bag
I'm a catatonic son of a bitch who's had
A touch too much of white powder

And she's a habit I can't handle
For a reason I can't say
I'm in love with a wild white lady
She's as sweet as the stories say
White powder white lady
You're one and the same
Come on down to my house wontcha
And hit this boy again

Shock waves to a tired brain
Sends that hungry lady to my door again
She's my shelter from the storm when I feel the rain
Entertaining white powder

I feel I'm dry-docked and tongue-tied
Heaven sends a stretcher for the kids to ride
I might just escape while the others might die
Ridin' on a high of white powder

white man danger

White man danger
He's come to stay
Red man, it's all over
You're in the way

White man danger
Time on his side
Red man, you don't know it
But your world just died

Let's hear it for the white man
He feels no pain
Let's hear it for the white man
Slim chance and none

White man danger
He's come to stay
Red man, it's all over
You're in the way

whitewash county

Tonight it's hot down here
I can almost smell the rain
And I can almost taste the fear
Behind your name
Fans turning on the ceiling
I feel sticky as a chilli dog
White boys howlin' in the evening
On that hollow log.

Tall tales down the river
Say we aim to bury the truth
But the right hand just delivered
The devil in a suit.

And he talks big in Whitewash County
Talks sweet as sugar cane
Gotta past that's filled with lightning
Gotta future filled with rain.

Bug buzzin' in an empty glass
Fiddle scratchin' some lazy tune
We're just some place that history passed
New dust, new broom
It's a high, hot buttered moon
He's got a shiny new wax face
Swears the South's gonna rise again soon
All over the place.

Tall tales down the river
Say we aim to bury the truth
But the right hand just delivered
The devil in a suit.

And he talks big in Whitewash County
Talks sweet as sugar cane
Gotta past that's filled with lightning
Gotta future filled with rain
Get on down.

. . . rain down on Whitewash County
Smell the air comin' up the line
Well you've changed your face so often
But you never change you mind.

who wears these shoes

There's a light on in your window
There's a shadow on the street
Two silhouettes tell me it's over
The shadow knows that shadow's me

I won't crawl or cause you trouble
That's the last thing I'll ever do
But before I leave your life completely
Tell me, who wears these shoes?

Lord knows the days just get longer
The nights grow cold with you on my mind
And I feel like an old jukebox
Playing the same song all the time

If these crazy dreams don't kill me
It's more than I can take from you
Not knowing where or when I'll see you
Not knowing darling who wears these shoes

My friends all say don't go to pieces
I say that's fine but if I lose
I wanna know who's in my footsteps
I wanna know who wears these shoes

My friends all think I must be crazy
I see the facts but if it's true
I wanna know who's in my footsteps
I wanna know who wears these shoes

And it's a chilling feeling
When I can't see him
What do I do
When I face the two of you
And it's a chilling feeling
When I can't see him
What do I do

wrap her up

These are ladies, illegal X's
Mona Lisa's, well connected

They may be shady, English roses
Blue blooded, turned up noses

Money talks, see what it catches
Postage paid, no strings attached

She's a honey, she's a tramp
Roaring twenties, molls and vamps

Wrap her up, I'll take her home with me
Wrap her up, she is all I need
Wrap her up, I only got one chance
Beasts and beauties, but they all can dance

Wrap her up, I'll take her home with me
Wrap her up, she is all I need
Wrap her up, give her to me
Wrap her up

Is she foreign, legs eleven
Italian girls, take me to heaven

You pretty babies, from Paris, France
Crazy horses, love to dance

Wrap her up, I'll take her home with me
Wrap her up, she is all I need
Wrap her up, I only got one chance
Beasts and beauties, but they all can dance

Wrap her up, I'll take her home with me
Wrap her up, she is all I need
Wrap her up, give her to me
Wrap her up

Give her to me, wrap her up
I'll take her home with me, wrap her up
She is all I need, wrap her up
I only got one chance, beasts and beauties
But they all can dance

Wrap her up, I'll take her home with me
Wrap her up, she is all I need
Wrap her up, give her to me

writing

Is there anything left?
Maybe steak and eggs.
Waking up to washing up,
Making up your bed.
Lazy days, my razor blade
Could use a better edge.

It's enough to make you laugh
Relax in a nice cool bath.
Inspiration for navigation
Of our new found craft.
I know you and you know me
It's always half and half.

And we were oh oh, so you know
Not the kind to doodle,
Will the things we wrote today
Sound as good tomorrow.
Will we still be writing?
In approaching years,
Stifling yawns on Sundays
As the weekends disappear.

We could stretch our legs if we'd half a mind
But don't disturb us if you hear us trying,
To instigate the structure of another line or two.
'Cause writing's lightin' up,
And I like life enough to see it through.

you gotta love someone

You can win the fight, you can grab a piece of the sky
You can break the rules but before you try
You gotta love someone
You gotta love someone

You can stop the world, steal the face from the moon
You can beat the clock but before high noon
You gotta love someone
You gotta love someone

You've got one life with a reason
You need two hearts on one side
When you stand alone and there's no one there
To share the way it feels inside – and baby

You can cheat the devil and slice a piece of the sun
Burn up the highway but before you run
You gotta love someone
You gotta love someone

When you're gonna play with fire
You let someone share the heat
When you're on your own and there's no one there
To cool the flames beneath your feet – and baby

You can win the fight, you can grab a piece of the sky
You can break the rules but before you try
You gotta love someone
You gotta love someone

you're so static

I've a constant ache in the morning light
It's on account of the night before
Some Park Lane lady in a shady bar
Took a fancy to the watch I wore.

But I can still remember how she laughed at me
As I spun around and hit the bed
She said 'Thank you honey, forget about the money
This pretty watch'll do instead.'

City living woman, you're so static
Matching your men with a hook and eye
If you're gonna spend the summer in New York City, Oh,
Them women Oh, Oh, Oh,
They're gonna slice your pie.

Said you're so static, baby I've had it
Rolling in a yellow cab
Downtown hustlers trying to pull some muscle
If they catch you, Oh, Oh, Oh, it could turn out bad.

It's 'Show me what you want, I'll show you what I've got
I can show you a real good time.'
She's a friend indeed, of a friend in need
But you'll be sorry when she leaves you cryin'.

your sister can't twist

I could really get off being in your shoes,
I used to be stone sold on rhythm and blues,
I heard of a place at the back of town
Where you really kick the shit when the sun goes down

I really got buzzed when your sister said:
'Throw away them records 'cause the blues is dead
Let me take you honey where the scene's on fire' —
And tonight I learned for certain that the blues
expired.

Oh your sister can't twist, but she can rock-and-roll.
Out bucks the broncos in the rodeo-do.
She's only sixteen, but it's plain to see
She can pull the wool over little old me.
Your sister can't twist but she can rock-and-roll
Your sister can't twist but she got more soul than me.

Somebody help me 'cause the bug bit me.
Now I'm in heaven with the aching feet.
But I'll be back tonight where the music plays —
And your sister rocks all my blues away.

Your Song

It's a little bit funny, this feeling inside
I'm not one of those, who can easily hide,
I don't have much money, but boy if I did
I'd buy a big house where we both could live.

If I was a sculptor, but then again no,
Or a man who makes potions in a travelling show
I know it's not much, but it's the best I can do
My gift is my song and this one's for you.

And you can tell everybody, this is your song
It may be quite simple but now that it's done,
I hope you don't mind, I hope you don't mind
That I put down in words
How wonderful life is while you're in the world.

I sat on the roof and kicked off the moss
Well a few of the verses, well they've got me quite cross
But the sun's been quite kind while I wrote this song,
It's for people like you, that keep it turned on.

So excuse me forgetting, but these things I do,
But you see I've forgotten, if they're green or they're blue
Anyway the thing is, what I really mean
Yours are the sweetest eyes I've ever seen.

ACKNOWLEDGEMENTS

p.5 photograph by Barrie Wentzell

p.8 'act of war' © 1985 Big Pig Music Ltd, UK
'a dandelion dies in the wind' reproduced by kind permission of Dick James Music Ltd
'all across the havens' reproduced by kind permission of Dick James Music Ltd
illustration by Fiona White

p.9. 'all quiet on the western front' © 1982 Big Pig Music Ltd, UK
illustration by Wherefore Art?

p.10. 'all the girls love alice' reproduced by kind permission of Dick James Music Ltd
illustration by Louise Kelly
'all the nasties' reproduced by kind permission of Dick James Music Ltd

p.11. 'amazes me' © 1989 Big Pig Music Ltd, UK
'amoreena' reproduced by kind permission of Dick James Music Ltd
'amy' reproduced by kind permission of Dick James Music Ltd
illustration by Dennis Leigh

p.12. 'angeline' © 1986 Big Pig Music Ltd, UK
'a word in spanish' © 1987 Big Pig Music Ltd, UK

p.13. 'bad side of the moon' reproduced by kind permission of Dick James Music Ltd
'ballad of a well-known gun' reproduced by kind permission of Dick James Music Ltd
illustration by Matthew Cooper

p.14. 'belfast' © 1994 Big Pig Music Ltd, UK
'believe' © 1994 Big Pig Music Ltd, UK

p.15. 'bennie and the jets' reproduced by kind permission of Dick James Music Ltd
photograph by Emerson Loew

p. 16. 'better off dead' © 1974 Big Pig Music Ltd, UK
'between seventeen and twenty' © 1976 Big Pig Music Ltd, UK

p.17. 'billie and the kids' © 1986 Big Pig Music Ltd, UK
'billy bones and the white bird' © 1975 Big Pig Music Ltd, UK
illustration by Charles Shearer

p.18. 'bite your lip (get up and dance!)' © 1975 Big Pig Music Ltd, UK
'bitter fingers' © 1974 Big Pig Music Ltd, UK
illustration by Paul Davis

p.19. 'blessed' © 1994 Big Pig Music Ltd, UK
photograph by Hag

p.20. 'blue avenue' © 1989 Big Pig Music Ltd, UK
'blues for my baby and me' reproduced by kind permission of Dick James Music Ltd
illustration by Graham Bence

p.21. 'boogie pilgrim' © 1976 Big Pig Music Ltd, UK
'border song' reproduced by kind permission of Dick James Music Ltd
'breaking hearts (ain't what it used to be)' © 1984 Big Pig Music Ltd, UK

p.22. 'burn down the mission' reproduced by kind permission of Dick James Music Ltd
p.23. 'burning buildings' © 1984 Big Pig Music Ltd, UK
illustrations by Liz Pyle

p.24. 'cage the songbird' © 1975 Big Pig Music Ltd, UK
'candle in the wind' reproduced by kind permission of Dick James Music Ltd
illustration by Mack Manning

p.26. 'candy by the pound' © 1985 Big Pig Music Ltd, UK
'can I put you on' reproduced by kind permission of Dick James Music Ltd

p.27. photograph by Peter Vernon

p.28. 'captain fantastic and the brown dirt cowboy' © 1974 Big Pig Music Ltd, UK
illustration by Janet Woolley

p.29. 'cartier' reproduced by kind permission of Dick James Music Ltd
'chameleon' © 1974 Big Pig Music Ltd, UK

p.30. 'chasing the crown' © 1980 Big Pig Music Ltd, UK
illustration by Archer Quinnell

p.31. 'club at the end of the street' © 1989 Big Pig Music Ltd, UK
illustration by Run Wrake

p.32. 'cold' © 1994 Big Pig Music Ltd, UK
'cold as christmas' © 1983 Big Pig Music Ltd, UK
'cold highway' © 1974 Big Pig Music Ltd, UK
illustration by Wherefore Art?

p.34. 'come down in time' reproduced by kind permission of Dick James Music Ltd
'country comfort' reproduced by kind permission of Dick James Music Ltd
illustration by Wherefore Art?

p.35. 'crazy water' © 1975 Big Pig Music Ltd, UK
illustration by Louise Brierly

p.36. 'crocodile rock' reproduced by kind permission of Dick James Music Ltd
illustration by Eduardo Paolozzi

p.37. 'cry to heaven' © 1986 Big Pig Music Ltd, UK
'crystal' © 1983 Big Pig Music Ltd, UK
'curtains' © 1974 Big Pig Music Ltd, UK
illustration by Joanne Foster

p.38. 'dancing in the end zone' © 1988 Big Pig Music Ltd, UK
illustration by Hannah Bryan

p.39. 'dan dare (pilot of the future)' © 1975 Big Pig Music Ltd, UK
Eagle Comics © Fleetway Editions Ltd, 1994

p.40. 'daniel' reproduced by kind permission of Dick James Music Ltd
illustration by Steve Wallace
'did he shoot her' © 1984 Big Pig Music Ltd, UK

p.41. 'dirty little girl' reproduced by kind permission of Dick James Music Ltd
'dixie lily' © 1974 Big Pig Music Ltd, UK
'don't go breaking my heart' © 1976 Big Pig Music Ltd, UK
illustrations by Hannah Bryan

p.42. 'don't let the sun go down on me' © 1974 Big Pig Music Ltd, UK
illustration by Michael Ross

p.43. 'durban deep' © 1989 Big Pig Music Ltd, UK
'easier to walk away' © 1990 Big Pig Music Ltd, UK

p.44-5. 'ego' © 1978 Big Pig Music Ltd, UK
illustrations by Huntley/Muir

p.169. 'tortured' © 1985 Big Pig Music Ltd, UK
painting by Derek Jarman courtesy Richard Salmon (London)

p.170. 'tower of babel' © 1974 Big Pig Music Ltd, UK
'town of plenty' © 1987 Big Pig Music Ltd, UK

p.171. 'two rooms at the end of the world' © 1980 Big Pig Music Ltd, UK
illustration by Wherefore Art?

p.172. 'understanding women' © 1991 Big Pig Music Ltd, UK
illustration by Catherine Denvir

p.174. 'valhalla' reproduced by kind permission of Dick James Music Ltd
'we all fall in love sometimes' © 1974 Big Pig Music Ltd, UK

p.175. 'western ford gateway' reproduced by kind permission of Dick James Music Ltd
illustration by Ruth Rowland

p.176. 'when a woman doesn't want you' © 1992 Big Pig Music Ltd, UK
'whenever you're ready (we'll go steady again)' reproduced by kind permission of Dick James Music Ltd

p.177. 'where have all the good times gone?' © 1982 Big Pig Music Ltd, UK
illustration by Anne Howeson

p.178. 'where's the shoorah?' © 1975 Big Pig Music Ltd, UK
p.179. 'where to now st. peter?' reproduced by kind permission of Dick James Music Ltd
illustration by Steve Wallace

p.180. 'whipping boy' © 1983 Big Pig Music Ltd, UK
'whispers' © 1988 Big Pig Music Ltd, UK

p.181. 'white lady white powder' © 1980 Big Pig Music Ltd, UK
illustration by Robin Cracknell
'white man danger' © 1980 Big Pig Music Ltd, UK

p.182. 'whitewash county' © 1992 Big Pig Music Ltd, UK
'who wears these shoes' © 1984 Big Pig Music Ltd, UK
'wrap her up' © 1985 Big Pig Music Ltd, UK

p.183. 'writing' © 1974 Big Pig Music Ltd, UK
photograph by Hag
'you gotta love someone' © 1990 Big Pig Music Ltd, UK

p.184. photograph by Herb Ritts

p.185. 'you're so static' © 1974 Big Pig Music Ltd, UK
'your sister can't twist' reproduced by kind permission of Dick James Music Ltd
illustrations by Mikey Georgeson

p.186. 'your song' reproduced by kind permission of Dick James Music Ltd
calligraphy by Ruth Rowland

p.187. photograph by Andy Kent

The illustrators listed above are the copyright holders of their work.

All songs written by Elton John and Bernie Taupin.

Big Pig Music Ltd., UK is represented by Warner Chappell Ltd., London WIY 3FA. Permission to reproduce the lyrics has been granted by International Music Publications Ltd.

The publishers acknowledge the support and cooperation in preparing this book received from Bernie Taupin and Michael Lippman in Los Angeles and Elton John, Steve Brown and Andrew Haydon at John Reid Enterprises.

The publishers further acknowledge the considerable achievements of the artists who have contributed to this volume and particularly appreciate the dexterity and design of Wherefore Art? and the art direction of David Costa. Wherefore Art? in turn would like to thank Fiona White for her invaluable assistance and would also like to acknowledge the expertise of both Tom Stanton (of East End Lights) and Mark Lewisohn.